AWESOME
ACTIVITY
BOOK

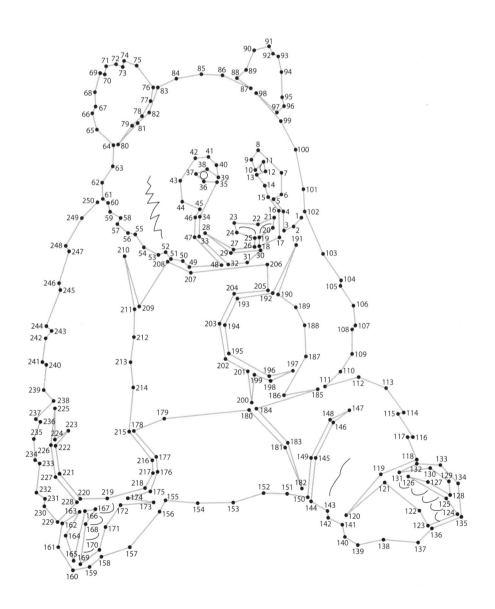

AWESOME ACTIVITY BOOK

INCLUDES WORD SEARCH, COLORING, DOT-TO-DOT, SUDOKU, AND CROSSWORDS

THUNDER BAY
P·R·E·S·S
San Diego, California

Thunder Bay Press
An imprint of Printers Row Publishing Group
9717 Pacific Heights Blvd, San Diego, CA 92121
www.thunderbaybooks.com • mail@thunderbaybooks.com

Printers Row Publishing Group is a division of Readerlink Distribution Services, LLC.
Thunder Bay Press is a registered trademark of Readerlink Distribution Services, LLC.

Correspondence regarding the content of this book should be sent to Thunder Bay Press, Editorial Department, at the above address. Author and rights inquiries should be addressed to Arcturus Holdings Limited, 26/27 Bickels Yard, 151-153 Bermondsey Street, London SE1 3HA, England; info@arcturuspublishing.com

Thunder Bay Press
Publisher: Peter Norton • Associate Publisher: Ana Parker
Editor: Dan Mansfield
Acquisitions Editor: Kathryn Chipinka Dalby

ISBN: 978-1-64517-994-8
CH010227US

Printed in China
25 24 23 22 21   1 2 3 4 5

INTRODUCTION

Welcome to this wonderful collection of activities! Take a little time out to relax and recharge your batteries by solving the puzzles and completing the dot-to-dot and coloring images within. This book contains a selection of fun activities to suit your mood—maybe you'll feel inspired to complete the beautiful coloring images, intrigued to see the pictures revealed magically by following the dots, or have a yearning to give your brain a gentle workout by tackling one of the popular number and word puzzles inside. Wherever you choose to start, settle down for some "me time" and have fun!

Here are some brief instructions in case any of the activities are new to you.

Word Search

Next to each grid is a list of all the words that can be found hidden in it, reading forward or backward, in either a horizontal, vertical, or diagonal direction, as with the example of the words APPLE, BANANA, ORANGE, PEAR, and PLUM, shown in the grid below:

Crosswords

Solve each clue and fill in the answer in the grid, with one letter in each square. If you are stuck on any answer, look at the words it intersects with, and try to solve those clues first, to give you some letters as a starting point.

Sudoku

Each sudoku puzzle starts with some numbers already in place and you need to fill in the remaining numbers, one per blank square, to complete it.

When finished, every horizontal row, vertical column, and 3x3 block of squares contains all of the numbers from 1 to 9, as with this example of a completed puzzle:

1	7	3	8	4	9	2	5	6
5	2	8	7	1	6	9	4	3
6	9	4	2	3	5	8	1	7
2	1	9	4	6	8	3	7	5
3	6	5	1	9	7	4	8	2
4	8	7	3	5	2	6	9	1
7	5	6	9	8	3	1	2	4
9	3	1	5	2	4	7	6	8
8	4	2	6	7	1	5	3	9

Dot-to-Dot

Find the number 1 in each dot-to-dot puzzle, then follow the numbers sequentially with your pencil or pen to reveal the hidden images.

Coloring

Choose your color combinations and use whatever medium works for you—felt pens, markers, gel pens, pencils, crayons—it's up to you.

Solutions

The solutions to the puzzles and dot-to-dots are to be found at the back of the book, but try not to peek!

WORD SEARCH
ROCKS AND MINERALS

```
E D E Z F T S S I E N G M E U
E T S G F E U Z M U O F U N T
L R A M U J T Z I N C G N O L
W H R N T A U L P R U D P O A
N D C O T R H T N I C A J G S
L A O C A H J O N Y X O S R A
P R D N I C R U L S E P N A B
Y C I N O M A A C I H Z Q J I
R T E N L D P Q C A V B W G I
E S P W B S S H L I O I Q A R
B N U A D A A E P R T Y N L E
V D M G Y L R P A U T E P E M
Z F I A K I H X U B N D A N A
Q U C T T I F T S I H C S A R
W Y E E M U S P Y G C I J N D
```

AGATE	GYPSUM	PUMICE
ANTHRACITE	IDOCRASE	SCHIST
BASALT	JACINTH	SPAR
BORAX	JARGOON	SPHALERITE
CHALK	JET	TUFF
COAL	MARL	URANITE
GALENA	OLIVINE	ZINC
GNEISS	ONYX	ZIRCON

SUDOKU

1	2	7		8				3
				2	3			9
			7					6
	7	3	4		5	9	6	
4		1				5		2
	8	9	2		6	7	1	
8					4			
9			3	5				
7				6		3	4	1

					9			1
8	4	9		2				7
			7	4				6
	2	6	1		4	9	8	
5		8				3		4
	9	7	3		5	6	1	
6				3	7			
9				1		7	5	8
2			5					

CROSSWORD

Across

1 Think ahead

5 Coined money

11 Art ___

12 Japanese name for Japan

13 Having widely applicable effects: hyph.

15 Perpetually cold level on a mountain

16 More sticky or viscous

20 Vowel sound in "lakes": 2 wds.

24 Quartet member

25 Slurpee rival

26 Country's McEntire

27 Scarlett's love

29 One-time Anaheim Stadium player, briefly: 2 wds.

30 Phoenician goddess of fertility

32 Middle of the day, old-style

37 Son of reggae star Bob, who sang "Tomorrow People": 2 wds.

40 Actress Renée of silent movies

41 Month before Sivan

42 Ancient Egyptian writing sheets

43 Without clothing

Down

1 Some transmittable files, initially

2 Tilt

3 Peak or tip: prefix

4 Neighbor of Swed.

5 Slow mover

6 Dine al fresco, maybe

7 Items of short-lived use

8 Economic stat.

9 Saturn model

10 He was attached to his brother

14 Murder suspect in "Lohengrin"

17 Robert who played A.J. Soprano

18 Island of Napoleon's exile

19 Gad about

20 Italy's currency, before the euro

21 Big name in newspaper publishing

22 Nair rival, once

23 Blow up: 2 wds.

28 Actor and comedian Verne

29 Singer Horne

31 "China Beach" actress Concetta

33 Tampa paper, familiarly

34 ___ Prigogine, 1977 winner of the Nobel Prize in Chemistry

35 Expensive

36 Thornfield governess

37 Microwave

38 Panhandle state: abbr.

39 Republicans, for short

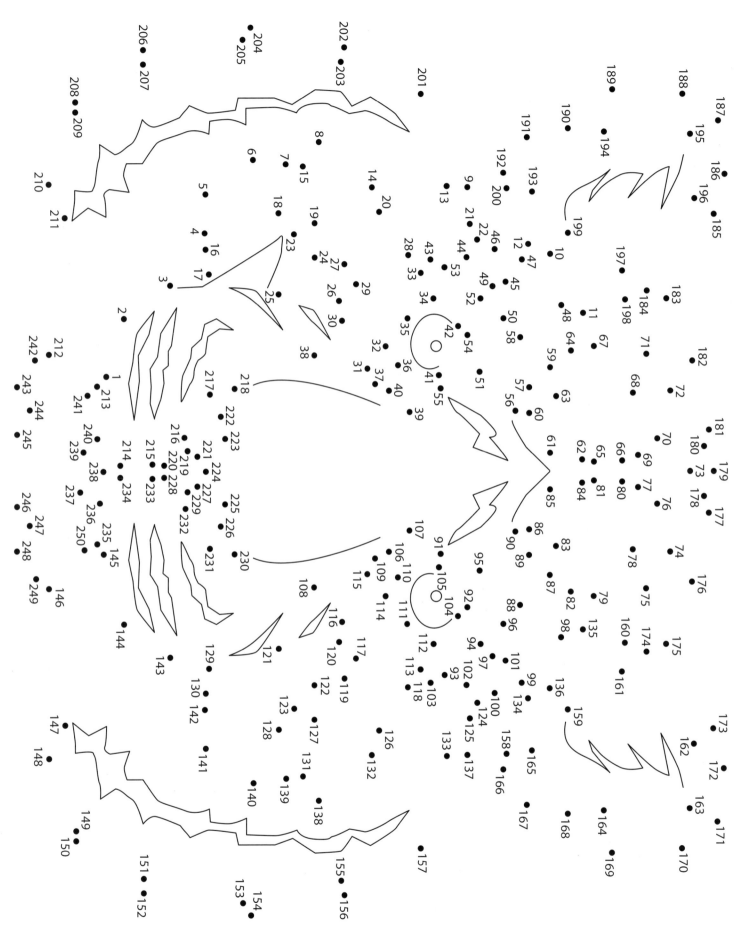

WORD SEARCH
VEGETABLES

```
U Y B R E T I I D C Q D A M S
V T C R S E L P A T L R G A S
F J P A L B N I K P M U P Y E
Z V E Y U R R M O S O O J O R
D K K S P E G T A G E G I J C
N K O Y L T A U F R C H A R D
H H H E Q M R B S H K U Z O S
I S C T O L L A H S Y O T O T
W J I T E W I L O F A N S S U
S O T D P C C X I P E V A S O
N J R G A K U S K I O E O G R
E C A R E R L T M A P T R Y P
E K T N A A H I T C L F A E S
R V V G S M P R I E P E D T A
G I Q R E W O L F I L U A C O
```

ARTICHOKE	KALE	PUMPKIN
CAULIFLOWER	LETTUCE	RADISH
CELERIAC	MARROW	SALSIFY
CHARD	OKRA	SAVOY
CRESS	PEAS	SHALLOT
GARLIC	PIMIENTO	SPROUTS
GOURD	POTATO	TOMATO
GREENS	PULSE	YAM

SUDOKU

	3		6		9	7		
	2		5		7	3	4	
		9		4				8
9		2			3		5	
	4			5			9	
	6		8			1		7
3				2		6		
	9	1	7		5		8	
		8	4		1		3	

		5	6			1		
6	2	3				5	7	9
	7		2	3			8	
	8				1	7		
7			5		9			2
		6	4				3	
	5			4	6		1	
9	6	7				2	4	8
		4			8	9		

CROSSWORD

Across

1 Putin's yeses
4 Highland fall
7 Suffix with president
10 "The Island of the Day Before" author
11 "Cool"
12 Windy City rail inits.
13 Athlete who plays for pay part-time: hyph.
15 Handy abbr.
16 "Alice's Adventures in Wonderland" creature: 2 wds.
18 China's Chou En-___
19 Initials on old Asian maps
20 Tree pollinated by bats
22 Fencing swords
25 Elbow
26 Rowboat needs
27 "Futurama" character with purple hair
29 Spice in curries
30 Laid up
31 Shakespeare's Bottom had the head of one
32 Picnickers run races in them: 2 wds.
37 Prince, initially
38 Beseech
39 French pope Urban II
40 Calf's cry
41 Suffix with ball or bass
42 Sponge
43 Airport abbr.
44 Compaq products, initially

Down

1 Fam. tree member
2 Banda ___ (Sumatran city)
3 1959 movie with Marilyn Monroe: 4 wds.
4 Actress Loren
5 "Me neither": 2 wds.
6 "___ with No Name" hit for America: 2 wds.
7 Baskin-Robbins tool: 3 wds.
8 "___ boy!"
9 Milk: prefix
14 Spanish queen who sponsored Columbus
17 Engagement, old-style
20 Two-stripe soldier, briefly
21 Want ad palindrome, initially
23 Son of Gad (Genesis 46:16)
24 Hirer's request letters
28 Mid-sized Nissan car
29 One of a religious trio
32 Light: prefix
33 Word on a dollar bill
34 Actor/bridge expert Sharif
35 "Grinding It Out" subject Ray
36 D.C. group

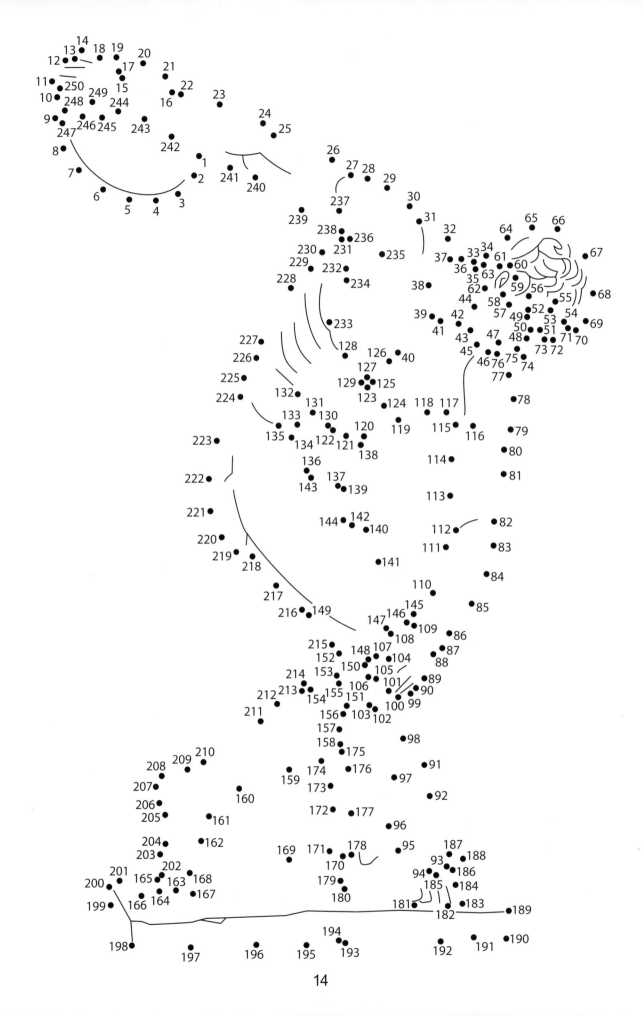

14

WORD SEARCH
ASTEROIDS AND MOONS

```
A F T I H R W R E L Z D X G V
S A L L A P G B S R J R U A M
S O B O H P E K G B O H M N L
I R S H A O E W Z Y D E R Y A
R Z H Y H V H T K A W A S M S
A E F P N Y Y T U H E A A E T
L R E E D J C M I S P L N D R
A P O R U E I M L P T E A E A
J L A I K R Q U H H L P I X E
E M P O A O H O E E O E N K A
J J A N U S M A H R T F A C J
T U D O T D I O T F Y H T U E
T A W I D N M I Z U H G I P P
B A S S A L A H T S Y H T E T
X A R O C Y S G F C T L X G I
```

AMALTHEA	IAPETUS	PORTIA
ASTRAEA	JANUS	PUCK
EROS	LARISSA	RHEA
EUROPA	MIMAS	SAPPHO
GANYMEDE	MIRANDA	SYCORAX
HELENE	PALLAS	TETHYS
HYDRA	PHOBOS	THALASSA
HYPERION	PHOEBE	TITANIA

SUDOKU

		9		8		3		
	4	3	5			1	8	
7		8			3	2		4
5	3		6	9				
	7						2	
				4	7		1	3
9		1	8			4		6
	6	7			2	8	5	
		5		1		9		

6	1			5			9	7
3				9				6
		4	3		6	1		
2	9		6		7		4	3
		6	5		4	9		
4	5		2		9		6	8
		7	9		3	8		
8				4				5
1	4			2			7	9

CROSSWORD

Across

1 Afflictions
5 Blunt
11 "Othello" author: abbr.
12 Algonquian tribe
13 Bon ___ ("Burning Bridges" band)
14 Southern Mexico state
15 Officially register on a course
17 Lord's worker
18 "___-Dabba-Doo!"
22 "___ ever wonder…": 2 wds.
23 Given an oath, with "in"
24 Farmer's area of study: abbr.
25 Rapa ___, native Polynesians of Easter Island
26 Early medium-range missiles
29 Pain relief choice
31 Ireland's patron, for short: 2 wds.
32 Lowly laborer
33 Cheerfulness
35 Floor-cleaning robot
38 Golden ager's org.
41 Like some non-permanent art exhibits: 2 wds.
42 Conductor Stravinsky
43 Joins together
44 Old Testament mountain

Down

1 Financial newspaper, for short
2 Palindromic expression of surprise
3 Listen surreptitiously
4 ___ latte (coffee choice)
5 Melville tale of the South Seas
6 Onion-topped bread rolls
7 C.P.A.'s concern: 2 wds.
8 Thurman of "Pulp Fiction"
9 Quotation qualification
10 What that is in Spain
16 New Deal prog.
17 Prime-time time
19 "Have a good journey": 2 wds.
20 UCLA player
21 Indigo
22 "Carmen Jones" song: "___ Love"
27 1950 hit for The Ames Brothers: 2 wds.
28 Take a ___ (attempt): 2 wds.
29 Donkey Kong or King Kong
30 Hold back
34 McEwan and Somerhalder
35 ___-A-Fella Records
36 Yoko of Beatles fame
37 Slangy intensifier
39 Rip off
40 One who plays for a living

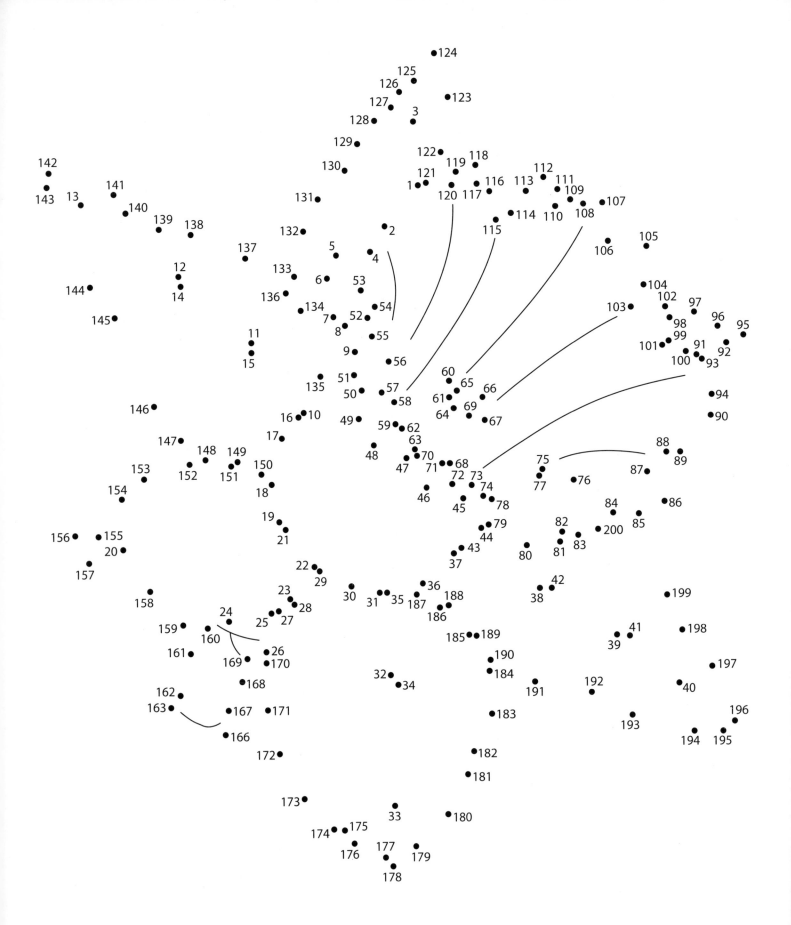

WORD SEARCH
STATES OF AMERICA

```
V S T T E S U H C A S S A M X
A J O P J T Q A M O N T A N A
I J H S A M A I N E V A D A A
N N A H R A S A L A V I T O N
I Q D J E S S I O N I L L I I
G N I M O Y W G Z I V D Q H L
R I C U N S A R C T I D N O O
I M R I A A O O M E Q A S I R
V I K S R K C E A X E F W G A
L K N R J S R G R A Y J C A C
F A A I N A V L Y S N N E P H
K N O M M L O K L A H O M A T
Y W P I T A O D A R O L O C R
A R M M Z K B P N J G K K G O
N O G E R O O V D V J A Y E N
```

ALASKA	MAINE	OHIO
COLORADO	MARYLAND	OKLAHOMA
GEORGIA	MASSA-	OREGON
HAWAII	CHUSETTS	PENNSYLVANIA
IDAHO	MISSOURI	TEXAS
ILLINOIS	MONTANA	UTAH
INDIANA	NEVADA	VIRGINIA
IOWA	NORTH	WYOMING
KANSAS	CAROLINA	

SUDOKU

5	8	1				7	2	9
	3		2	7			8	
		6	9			1		
		8			6		3	
2			1		5			8
	7		4			9		
		5			3	4		
	6			4	9		1	
3	4	2				8	9	5

		6			5			
		3		2		9	5	1
		7	1	4				
7	6		8		2		9	3
9		5				8		4
1	3		5		4		2	7
				8	1	7		
3	8	9		6		1		
			3			2		

CROSSWORD

Across

1 Aura

7 Letters identifying a combination of voices (music)

11 Framework of metal bars used as a partition

12 "Good buddy"

13 Writer Fallaci

14 Assyrian place of exile mentioned in the Bible

15 Painkilling drug

17 Classic board game

20 HBO alternative

21 Eddie's "Coming to America" role

23 "Be-Bop-___" (1956 Gene Vincent hit): hyph.

27 Calvin on the links

28 One sporting three stars: abbr., 2 wds.

29 From Nineveh: abbr.

30 "That '70s Show" role for Kutcher

31 Letters accompanying some 2,000-year-old+ dates

33 Isles

34 Bearing in abundance

38 Meter maid of song

39 Pakistani city

43 PC pic

44 Difference in years between people: 2 wds.

45 Covering to conceal the face

46 Some sculptures

Down

1 Aid group, often: initials

2 Flawed somehow: abbr.

3 1002, to Cicero

4 Euphemism for "damn", e.g.: hyph.

5 Arm part

6 Cooks over high heat

7 Certain educator

8 Blind as ___: 2 wds.

9 Hatcher of "Desperate Housewives"

10 Bric-a-___

16 Stick used in a classroom

17 ___ Nui (Easter Island)

18 Turner and others

19 Takes out

22 French word for "thank you"

24 Appropriately named fruit

25 "___ we forget"

26 Parts of una década

32 Key of Beethoven's "Eroica": 2 wds.

34 Prudish

35 Costa ___

36 Oklahoma tribe

37 Othello's betrayer

40 Old-school tough guys in rap songs, initially

41 Dileep who played Yusuf in "Inception"

42 Some song releases, typically: inits.

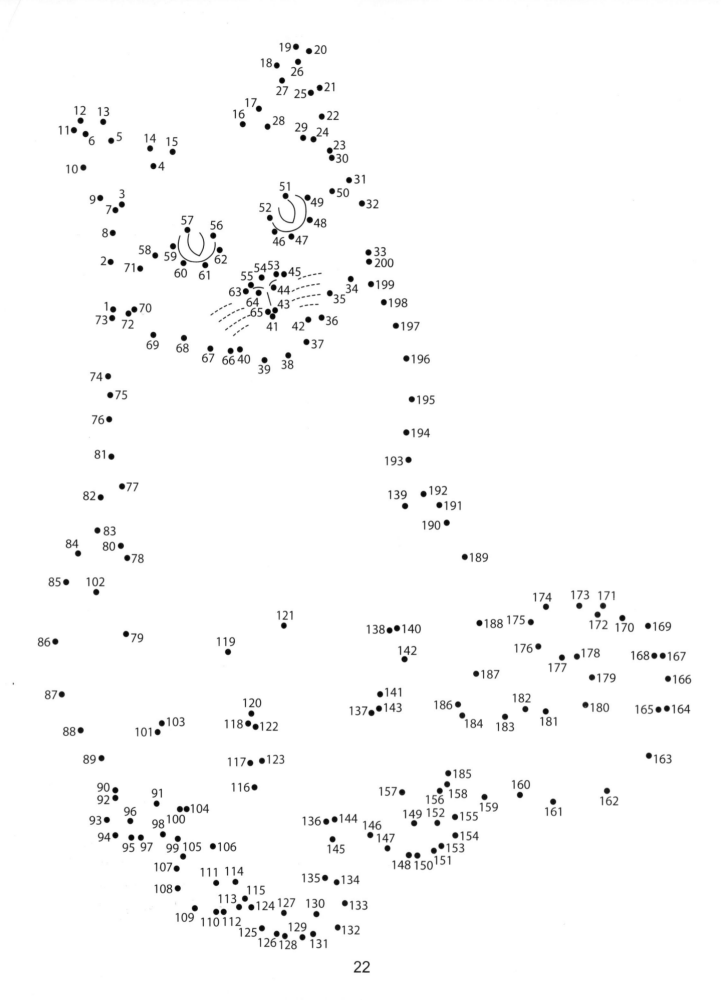

22

WORD SEARCH
CALENDAR

```
R Z W J H I P W W P F J K K Q
E E U C N O V E M B E R U O Z
X N R F R I D A Y S L C J L G
E A T K M N V A P R I L V W Y
M V Z H E A R E B M E T P E S
D V M S U Z J A N U A R Y E K
K U D G O R F K Z Y R E A K A
X A U M U I S S A L A B D E H
Y S R Q R H R D T L E O R N O
T M C E G A N U A U Y T U D L
R O E Q T O E A Z Y W C T D I
T N C S M S R M A V E O A M D
Q T E R D N A Y A D N U S O A
L H V A W Y R E B M E C E D Y
I S Y C H R I S T M A S F W N
```

APRIL	JULY	OCTOBER
AUGUST	JUNE	SATURDAY
CHRISTMAS	MARCH	SEPTEMBER
DECEMBER	MAY	SUNDAY
EASTER	MONDAY	THURSDAY
FRIDAY	MONTHS	TUESDAY
HOLIDAY	NEW YEAR	WEDNESDAY
JANUARY	NOVEMBER	WEEKEND

SUDOKU

9			7	1		4		8
	4				3	1		
5					9	7	6	
		5		8			4	7
	8		9		7		3	
2	1			3		9		
	3	9	4					2
		6	2				7	
4		2		6	1			5

			1	9		2	5	
	9		8		7			1
6	3				5		7	
		2	6	7		9		
	6	4				2	1	
		7		2	1	3		
	8		1				6	3
5			4		6		8	
1	2		7	3				

24

CROSSWORD

Across

1 Stinger
5 Rust, e.g.
10 City east of Santa Barbara
11 Animals' scent trails
12 Aladdin's shiner
13 Ball
14 Milk shake made with ice cream
16 Big ref. works, for short
17 Straightforward
19 "Give ___ rest!": 2 wds.
21 Worship
25 Skye cap
26 Hospital V.I.P.s
27 Super ___ (GameCube predecessor)
28 Polite response: 2 wds.
30 Japanese computer giant, initially
31 Proximo's opposite
33 Hussy
36 Emotionally unavailable type
39 Disc jockey's favorites: 2 wds.
41 Alway's antonym
42 Suitable for all audiences: 2 wds.
43 Old ExxonMobil brand name
44 Traditional nighttime campfire treat
45 Roman emperor after Galba

Down

1 Jackal's kin
2 Close to closed
3 Patriot for whom a beer is named: 2 wds.
4 Astrid Lindgren character, ___ Longstocking
5 Unlock, poetically
6 Aztec god who guided the dead to Mictlan
7 Woman abducted by Hercules
8 Scott who sued to end his own slavery
9 Calculates roughly: abbr.
11 One way to find a partner: 2 wds.
15 First
18 Characteristic of the universe
19 Suffix with odd or complex
20 ___-Bo (exercise system)
22 Free from guilt
23 End of a series
24 Upper-left key
29 Talk under one's breath
32 "Rebel Without a Cause" costar Sal
33 Orch. section
34 Gardener's bagful
35 "It's ___ you" ("Not my decision"): 2 wds.
37 Solidarnosc name
38 Ending for smack or smash
40 Dutch city

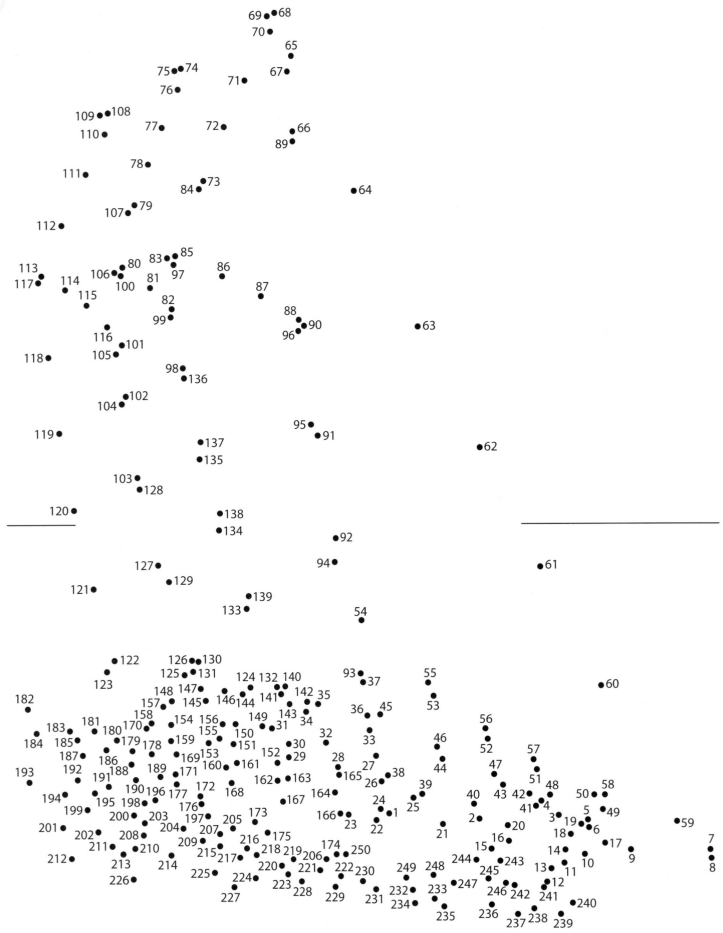

26

WORD SEARCH
PUNCTUATION MARKS AND SIGNS

```
M T A A M R J N D O I R E P F
A N N O R B G Z O D O Y V Y C
C I O K R A M N O I T S E U Q
R O I F W U A W C B S I V O Q
O P T H H C E O O Q L I L Q D
N L A T E A L K M Q L I V D H
U A C I H O S A M Y U J Q I E
F M I C N E C T A M U E N U D
P I L K M C R N E Q Y K S S E
L C P A E U K E H R C H A S H
D E I N U G M Y F A I P Q L S
N D T T A T P V R O M S L A A
U Y L J D H Z E C A R B K U D
O Z U H E V T U I T E E U Q S
P M M N H O T P S S Y O D E R
```

ACCENT	DIVISION	PERIOD
ASTERISK	EQUALS	PLUS
BRACE	EURO	POUND
CARET	HASH	QUESTION
COLON	HYPHEN	MARK
COMMA	MACRON	THEREFORE
DASH	MULTIPLICATION	TICK
DECIMAL POINT	OBLIQUE	TILDE
		UMLAUT

SUDOKU

			8	5				9
2	5	7		1				8
					7			6
	7	8	4		3	9	6	
3		2				4		5
	1	9	6		5	7	2	
1			3					
7				6		8	3	2
9				4	8			

4		3					1	
	2	6		4			9	7
			1	6	5			
2	3	5	4					9
		4	6		2	1		
7					9	2	4	8
			2	8	6			
5	1			9		6	7	
	9					4		3

CROSSWORD

Across

1. ___ control
5. Lollipop cop of 1970s and 1980s TV
10. Former Indy champ Bobby
12. Draw forth
13. Russian vodka brand, for short
14. "Fiddler on the Roof" matchmaker
15. Girl, historically
17. "Whom have ___ heaven but you?" Psalms 73:25: 2 wds.
18. Boardroom bigwig, initially
20. "Arjuna's Dilemma" composer Douglas J.
22. Radio switch: hyph.
24. Unclear
27. Simpson, Bonet and Vanderpump
29. Santa's little helpers
30. Menial
32. Idle
33. Gem made by an animal
35. Computer file format, initially
36. Veterinary anesthetic, initially
38. Exams for aspiring D.A.s
40. "Take ___ off!" ("Relax!"): 2 wds.
42. Bake, as eggs
45. Bouquet ___
46. Urge to attack: 2 wds.
47. ___ nerve (eye part)
48. Court official's cry: var.

Down

1. Sets of two, briefly
2. Take in food
3. Donation, perhaps: 3 wds.
4. Yarn
5. Garment's decorative cutout
6. Poem that praises
7. B team: 2 wds.
8. Start of a play: 2 wds.
9. Razor-sharp
11. "The Mod Squad" detective
16. Green reporter
18. Young seal
19. Actor Jannings
21. Large island of the Inner Hebrides, Scotland
23. Lion's hair
25. Iran's ___ Shah Pahlavi
26. Scene of heavy WWI fighting
28. Relating to old Norse poetry
31. Calendar spans: abbr.
34. Lad's love
36. When doubled, the chief port of American Samoa
37. Show appreciation
39. Only Huxtable boy
41. Folk rocker DiFranco
43. Kind of deer
44. M.D. colleagues

WORD SEARCH
WILD WEST

```
C V O Y S E M A J E S S E J O
S B M S S A H P K G T R H N L
R O B T S H M O L Q E O S L Z
E U E P O A P B R P E D U Y Z
L N L W U W L E A S R E R A N
B T D I O D S L O S E O D D O
M Y D C O S N A R Q S S L I S
A J A A O H U U L Q K C O L T
G X S P U R S N O O Y M G L E
T T O Y R N H N N R O H M O T
A A S T A M P E D E J N W H S
F F B U F M E F D R X I C C H
F E Q P Z A D N V F N N Q O T
Q C F E G M A R S H A L L D Y
W I L D B U N C H R I A H Q V
```

BOUNTY	JESSE JAMES	SALOON
COWPOKE	LASSO	SAM BASS
DEPUTY	MARSHAL	SPURS
DOC HOLLIDAY	POSSE	STAMPEDE
GAMBLER	RANCH	STEER
GOLD RUSH	RODEO	STETSON
HORSES	ROUNDUP	TOM HORN
HOWDY	SADDLE	WILD BUNCH

SUDOKU

		2	8		6			4
6					9	5		7
3		9		2	4			
	7			3	2		6	
2	3						1	5
	4		5	6			3	
			6	7		2		3
5		7	2					8
8			1		5	9		

7					1		3	4
1	4	9	3					
	2			6	5	7		
5				8		2	4	
9			6		2			5
	7	1		4				8
		8	7	2			9	
					4	5	8	7
3	1		8					6

CROSSWORD

Across

1 Contribution of work or information
6 Dudgeon
11 Writer Zora ___ Hurston
12 "Be-Bop-___" (1956 Gene Vincent hit): hyph.
13 Seat of Silver Bow County, Montana
14 University heads
15 Suffix with cap or coy
16 First word of Dante's "Inferno"
18 "Can't Help Lovin' ___ Man" (Ella Fitzgerald)
19 Part of E.T.A.: abbr.
20 ___-cone (cooler)
21 Hi-___ monitor
22 "Highly amusing!" in textspeak
24 Start for a playwright: 2 wds.
26 Enzyme that breaks down genetic material
28 Tenth letter of the Greek alphabet
31 Think (over)
33 Trout tempter
34 ASCAP's counterpart
36 Ending with mater or pater
38 Stephen of "The Crying Game"
39 Potent or penitent ending
40 "Am ___ risk?": 2 wds.
41 One-time MTV afternoon show
42 Vegetable that makes you cry
44 Car insurer, initially
46 Rihanna song of 2009: 2 wds.
47 Children's author Eleanor
48 Dolts
49 Has got to have

Down

1 Boat's engine housed inside its hull
2 Elementary particle
3 Male head of the household
4 Like the letter Z: abbr.
5 Parenting challenges
6 Security device
7 Suffix with percent
8 Involving four parties
9 Carpi connectors
10 Bridge seats
17 Old Spanish queen
23 Its captain is Mike the Tiger: inits.
25 Can opener
27 Weather-affecting currents: 2 wds.
29 Run through
30 Clueless: 3 wds.
32 When doubled, a yellow Teletubby
34 Regional flora and fauna
35 Flowing tresses
37 Sporter of three stars: abbr., 2 wds.
43 Cockney dwelling
45 Ending for legal or Senegal

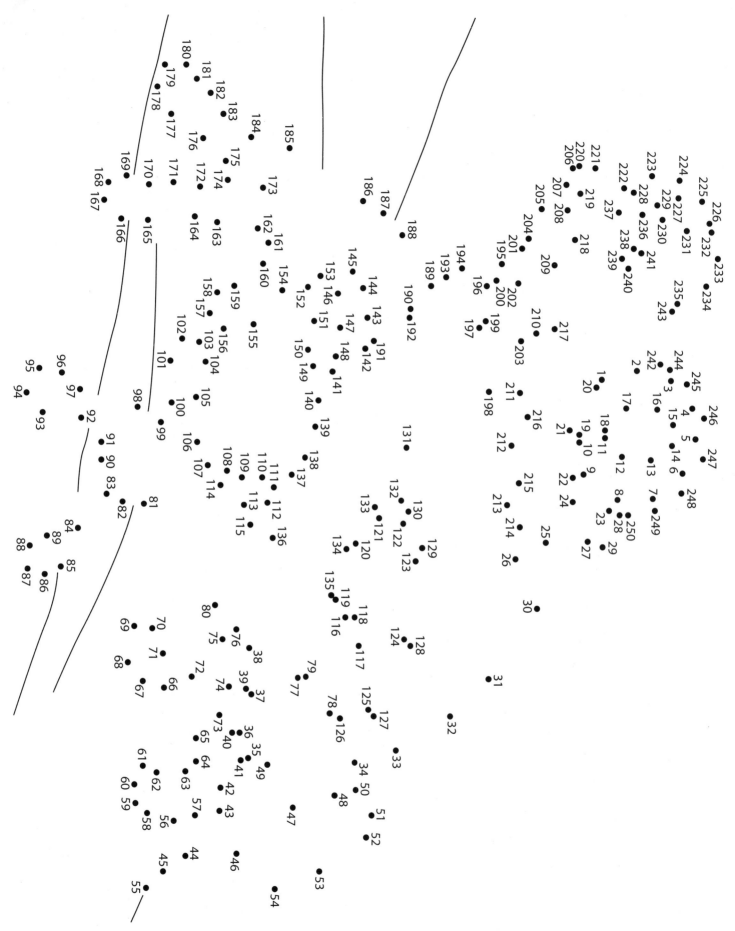

WORD SEARCH
THINGS THAT GO AROUND

```
E E H Y C F R T E N A L P F P
G Z Q O D R E I D E L V S W I
G I M B P L A H T R A E E H T
Y E R D W H E E L R D A C E R
T E Q M W C Q A O A T O N E L
G L O H A P S T L H M I L D E
J O I S L T O B E P B L K L S
N S T U E R R R U R E L E A U
K O N R F E V T U P Y H S Z O
R E O X W A E T O Z L J D Y R
T I H O N R N R Y L Z R O S A
D P M E D J P B I J O Y C U C
R G R I N D E R E C V K C S Y
Z Z S P I N D L E L J N Q A B
A K R O D A N R O T T P O N A
```

ASTEROID	GRINDER	SPINDLE
CAROUSEL	LAZY SUSAN	THE EARTH
CASTOR	MOON	TORNADO
COMET	MOWER BLADES	TURBINE
COMPUTER DISK	PLANET	WEATHER VANE
DREIDEL	PROPELLER	WHEEL
DRILL	RECORD	WHISK
FAN BELT	ROTOR	YO-YO

SUDOKU

		9				8		1
7			1		8			2
	1	6	9	7				4
	8	5		3	1			
	7		2		5		6	
			6	9		4	5	
5				4	3	9	1	
4			5		6			7
3		8				2		

5	9	7	4					
		2			9	6	8	
	1			3	7			9
3	4			9		5		
		5	3		2	1		
		9		4			7	8
7			5	2			3	
	6	4	8			7		
					6	8	4	1

CROSSWORD

Across

1 Nursery napping place
5 National insurance company
11 Popular tea
12 Art deco sculptor John
13 Kind of force
15 Fusilli or farfalle
16 Corporate image
17 Verdi aria sung by Renato: 2 wds.
20 Filmmaker Joel or Ethan
23 Absorb (liquid) with a cloth: 2 wds.
27 Bookmarked address, briefly
28 Signal at Sotheby's
29 California-based clothing brand, initially
30 Uproar
32 Hr. divs.
33 King Arthur's father
35 Univ. lecturer
38 Knight's need
42 Paris landmark: 2 wds.
45 Lamentation
46 Light and insubstantial (poetic)
47 Flowering plants of the tropics
48 Brit. decorations

Down

1 Letters on a Soyuz rocket
2 Funny Caroline
3 Fleming and Ziering
4 "Once ___, twice shy"
5 Fed. assistance program
6 Raiding grp.
7 Mistake that leads to confusion: hyph.
8 Start of a conclusion
9 Rock outcropping
10 Frogner Park's home
14 Data compression format letters
18 1976 Stevie Wonder chart-topper: 2 wds.
19 Prescription instruction, initially
20 "Dirty dog"
21 Tulsa sch. with a Prayer Tower
22 Stately tree
24 Ransom ___ Olds
25 Tea server
26 Some film ratings, initially
28 On the other hand
31 Hole-nesting auk
32 "The Wind in the Willows" character: 2 wds.
34 Superlative finale
35 Perks (up)
36 Make mad
37 End ___ era: 2 wds.
39 Rams' ma'ams
40 Architect Saarinen who designed the TWA Flight Center at JFK
41 Teetotalers
43 Bambi's aunt
44 Capt.'s inferiors

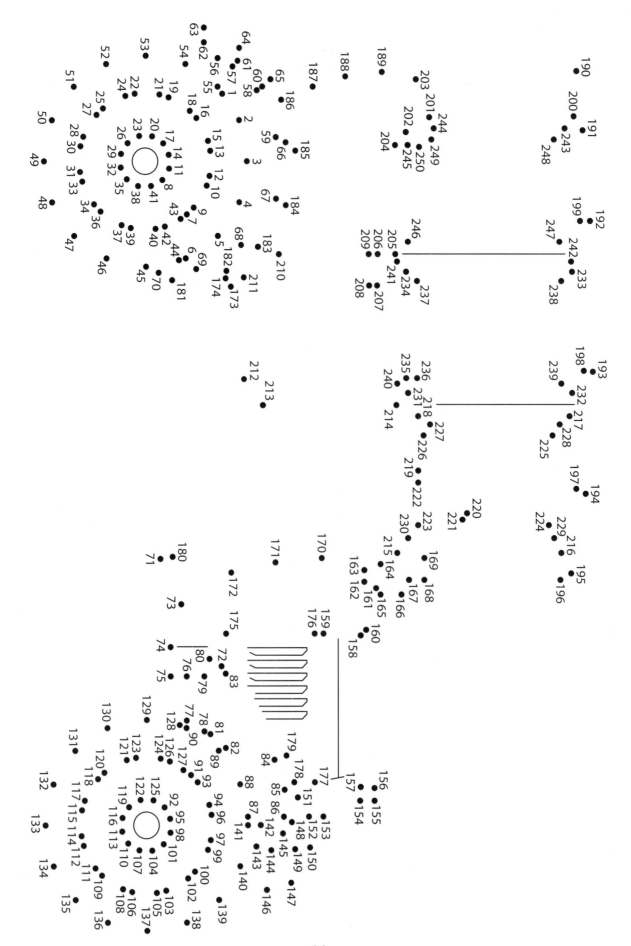

WORD SEARCH
"TAIL" ENDINGS

```
Y E L L O W T A I L M T K R C
H J X E I L I A T E V O D Y N
L B A A H A I R T A I L L W D
K I D M C O T T O N T A I L S
L P A L I A T E T I H W A I W
L I A T N E D K L X O G T A A
G G A D H E K L H T B S G T L
A T C T T S I L L S P N R L L
L A D A N A I G I I B I I U O
B I I Z T A L F A A A N R C W
O L A T T F F X T T W T L B T
L I A T K C A L B G K A E M A
W O A N X N H P O A A I M R I
C R G M U O H D B W K L J X L
D U C K T A I L I A T P I H W
```

BLACKTAIL	DUCKTAIL	RATTAIL
BOBTAIL	ENTAIL	RETAIL
BRISTLETAIL	FANTAIL	RINGTAIL
COATTAIL	FISHTAIL	SWALLOWTAIL
COTTONTAIL	HAIRTAIL	WAGTAIL
CURTAIL	OXTAIL	WHIPTAIL
DETAIL	PIGTAIL	WHITETAIL
DOVETAIL	PINTAIL	YELLOWTAIL

SUDOKU

5			4		6	2		
2			8		1	4		9
		3		7			5	
	1	4			2			3
9				8				6
8			5			7	9	
	2			6		9		
6		5	1		8			7
		1	9		3			5

				3	4	9		7
		4	1		8			3
2		5			7	8		
	8			9	3		5	
	6	2				3	9	
	9		2	8			4	
		1	3			2		5
7			6			2	1	
3		9	8	5				

CROSSWORD

Across

1 ___ buco (Italian dish)
5 Nolan Ryan, notably
10 Sitcom's Mork or Orson, e.g.
11 Decoy or siren, essentially
12 Certain Oldsmobile
13 Persona non ___
14 Pedicure target
15 Like some humor
17 Computer key next to the space bar
18 Org. for dentists
19 Barbecue site
20 Ditch
22 Reading rooms
23 Part of a giggle
24 Military address
25 New Mexico resort
27 Musical scale with no sharps or flats: 2 wds.
30 Ab ___ (from the beginning)
31 1949 film noir classic: inits.
32 "Now I see!"
33 Expresses disapproval: hyph.
35 Have, in Edinburgh
36 Cuban kid ___ González in 2000 headlines
37 Art giant Matisse
39 "Morning Joe" airer
40 "Tar Beach" author Richard
41 Transition
42 Country addresses, for short

Down

1 Baltimore base-stealer or bunter
2 Popular sport with clay targets: 2 wds.
3 Patriotic org.
4 How many dumb things are performed: 3 wds.
5 Pond owner's bane
6 Irrational number in math
7 Show spun off of "M*A*S*H": 3 wds.
8 Keep possession of
9 Praying figures
10 Set of eight things
16 Absorb, as a cost
21 Suffix with adopt or address
22 One day in Spain
24 Atom ___ (particle accelerator)
25 Native American symbols
26 Tear apart
27 Plain narrow bed
28 Margaret Mitchell family
29 German river
31 Chucklehead
34 Popular fragrance
38 One of Santa's Little Helpers

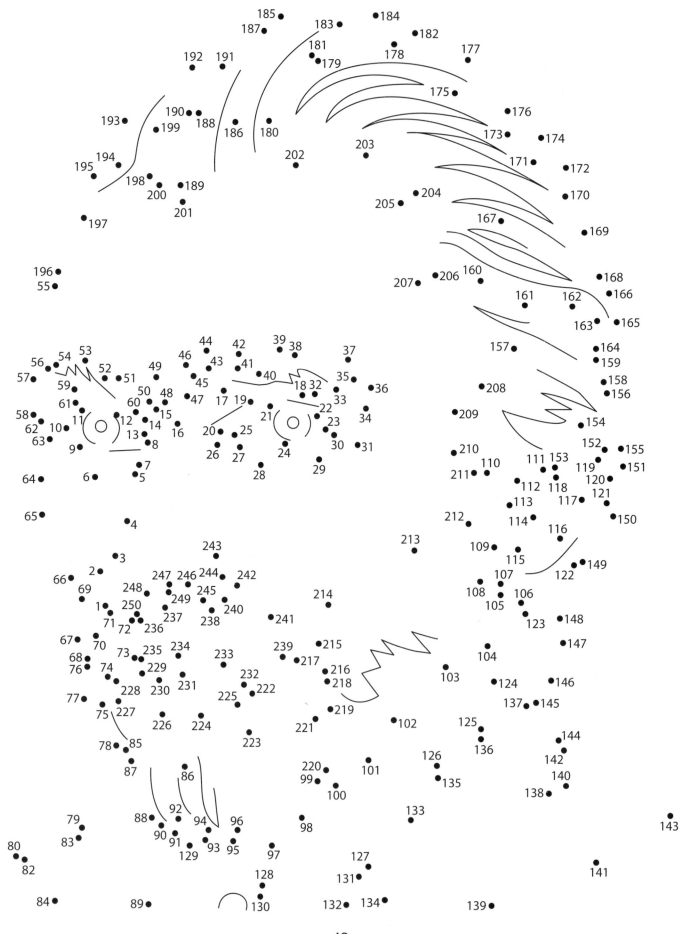

WORD SEARCH
SHADES OF BLUE

```
R O Y A L V E B O Q I G D K U
F B C K T F F S N I N D I G O
D I K O S U R R I T E A L U V
T R C L L M F E Y O I B K V D
I D O O O U W T N V U B V E P
F S C F H A M C S H Q N I D
F U A Y X Q E B G I H I R N Z
A D E C Y O R N I G M D L U T
N D P V O E U S Y A X N E K T
Y D A V O B Z B P G C O E A F
E N I R A M A U Q A Y B T D K
E C I L A B Q L T H A M S R R
F O J H G R T G T R N L A Z I
A I D P D U U H P P U D E I B
S E L K N I W I R E P E W L Z
```

ALICE	DARK	ROYAL
AQUAMARINE	DENIM	SKY
AZURE	FRENCH	STEEL
BABY	INDIGO	TEAL
BONDI	NAVY	TIFFANY
COBALT	OXFORD	TRUE
COLUMBIA	PEACOCK	TUFTS
CYAN	PERIWINKLE	TURQUOISE

SUDOKU

		1	3		6		9	
9				4		7		
	2	6	5		8		1	
2		4			9		8	
	3			8			2	
	7		1			6		5
	4		8		5	9	3	
		2		3				1
	9		7		2	5		

		7			6		3	4
5		9	2			1		
1				8	5		6	
8	9	1	4	7				
3								2
				6	9	7	8	1
	2		5	4				3
		5			3	8		7
7	4		9			6		

CROSSWORD

Across

1 Covered in folds of cloth

7 Newtons' filling

10 Common solvent

11 Johannesburg country, initially

12 Chinese vegetable: 2 wds.

14 Loud, as a crowd

15 Women's magazine, for short

16 Stone paving block

17 Some Art Deco works

18 Possess, in Scotland

19 Think carefully about

21 Packed like sardines

23 Handy-andies: hyph.

24 Watch chain

27 Plant with laxative properties

28 Smoke channel

29 Subsequently

30 2003 Mazda roadster

31 Fourth of July popper

33 "Telephone Line" grp.

34 Flighty scatterbrained simpleton (slang)

35 Salt, in Strasbourg

36 Least healthy-looking

Down

1 Beltway environs, briefly: 2 wds.

2 Channel changer: 2 wds.

3 In the box: 2 wds.

4 Lousy

5 "Another Green World" musician

6 Comes down

7 Kellogg's breakfast cereal: 2 wds.

8 Chemical cousin

9 Los ___ (city in western CA)

10 Flummox

13 Mob

19 Region of ice: 2 wds.

20 Night bird

22 Indian title: var.

23 Damage the purity or appearance of

25 Consume more than

26 Santa's trademark

27 Vaults

28 Flat sheet of microfilm, familiarly

30 Clay-lime mixture

32 River inlet

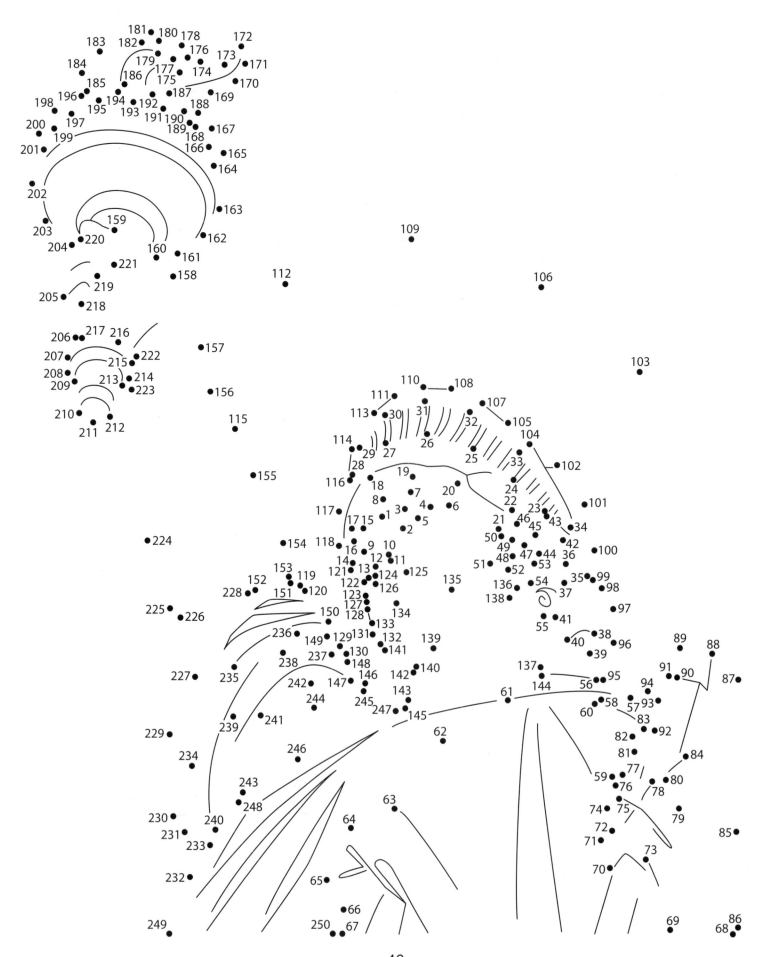

WORD SEARCH
CALM DOWN

```
R T Z G C B Y C H I L L O U T
A L L A Y F D S Y E E X E T D
C O N C I L I A T E S T I L L
W B S L E T M S E R S A N N E
K K L W A E I U M E E B M E T
N O A R C L N B P P N A M K A
M N E L O L I D E O V T J C R
E E L D O U S U R S Y E L A E
A C Q A L P H E Y E U A T L D
S N U W O I U F U P S F U S O
E E I N F P I P A S B Y E W M
O L E S F C A E U B Y H I D A
F I T X A P L A C A T E U I D
F S E P P F G T Q U E L L S B
Z T N X D E U Q B T A R M U H
```

ABATE	EASE OFF	QUIETEN
ALLAY	HUSH	REPOSE
ASSUAGE	LESSEN	SILENCE
CHILL OUT	MODERATE	SLACKEN
CONCILIATE	MOLLIFY	STILL
COOL OFF	PACIFY	SUBDUE
DEFUSE	PLACATE	TEMPER
DIMINISH	QUELL	WANE

SUDOKU

	9				4	1	2	
5		3	8				7	
8			1	6		9		
				7	3	6	9	2
		4				5		
6	7	9	2	8				
		5		3	1			4
	8				2	7		3
	6	7	5				1	

2	9	3	5					
		1		2			6	5
6	7			9	4			8
		4		3	1			
	3	8				5	7	
			7	8		4		
5			9	7			3	1
8	2			1		7		
					6	2	9	4

CROSSWORD

Across

1 Shirt feature

7 Dugout shelter

11 Indolent

12 One hundred dinars

13 With unwillingness

15 Rigid circular necklace that is open-ended at the front

16 Chai or chamomile

17 Alexander the Great's tutor

21 Fortune

22 British prince born in 2013

25 Certain condiment's origin: 2 wds.

28 Navy builder

29 Sparks on the screen

30 Prophetess whose warnings about the Trojan Horse went unheeded

33 Hindustani Mr.

35 "This ___" (Randy Travis album): 2 wds.

36 Makes a donation

41 Starter letters

42 Truth

43 Kind of scale

44 Water or wind, e.g.

Down

1 ___ anglais (English horn)

2 Suffix with Capri

3 Count Basie's "___ Darlin'"

4 Clumsy oafs

5 Fancy tie

6 Going backward

7 "Prince Valiant" character

8 Final unpleasant moment: 2 wds.

9 Crackling sound

10 ___ Prigogine, Nobel Prize-winning physicist

14 Functioned

17 Charity

18 Philandering fellow

19 "Easy as pie!": 3 wds.

20 ___ Angeles Lakers

23 Will ___, Grandpa Walton portrayer

24 Mythology anthology

26 Not yet decided, initially

27 Norse deities collectively

31 Resin from ancient trees

32 Prefix with surgery or transmitter

33 Fast one

34 Cop or call prefix

37 Highly successful kickoff returns: abbr.

38 Rx instruction, initially

39 Somme time

40 Country whose capital is Damascus: abbr.

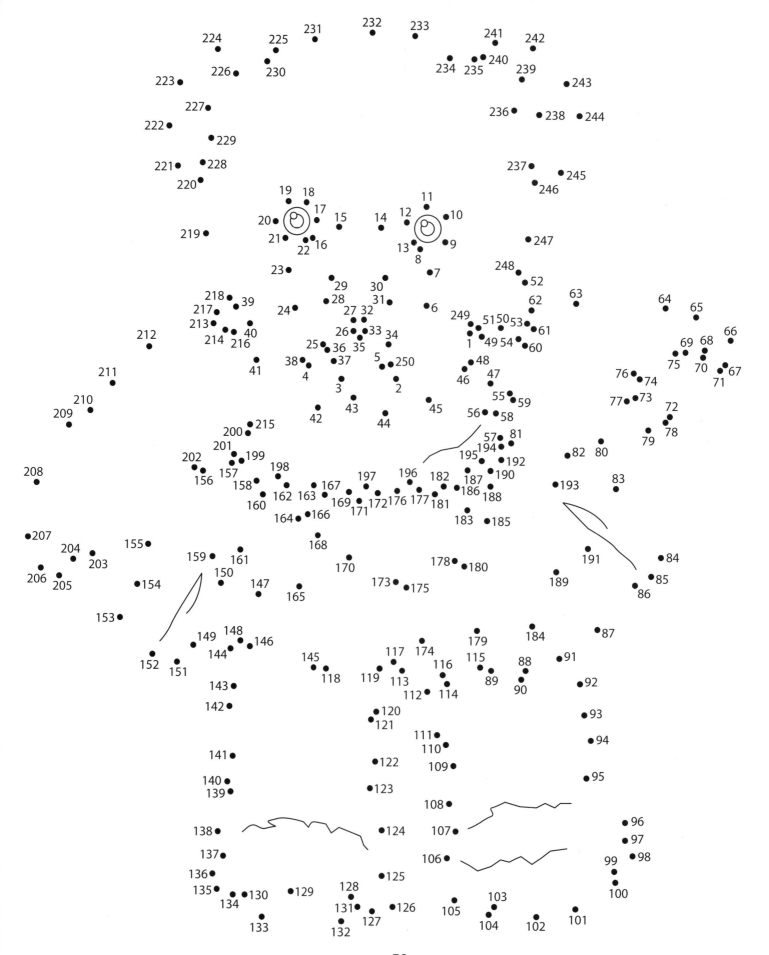

WORD SEARCH
LUMPS AND BUMPS

```
O R E C E I P D H S M B R R T
M H G Q I D A G Y S E P C J O
C L U M P W O O R H A U Y Y Q
B X N D G A K N O O B B M K O
M W W B O W M A E B W G L N S
L H U I E L K A P U S T U L E
M R K D G Z C P S L W X H I L
R V G N E C N E C S E R C X E
T E A Y R U J N I E K B X P T
P R B S C T D U T I L N A Y B
L M G U L S G G K S X U U L I
O L U L T Q K G N C V M D R L
B S D H O U O E A A O J W O C
B C A L N L I T I S C L O T N
F P P R O J E C T I O N B G I
```

BALL	GROWTH	PIECE
BLOCK	HUMP	PROJECTION
BURR	INJURY	PUSTULE
CLOD	KNUR	SLUB
CLOT	MASS	SLUG
CLUMP	NODE	TUBER
EXCRESCENCE	NODULE	WAD
GNARL	NUGGET	WEDGE

SUDOKU

		1	6		2	9		
8				9				5
	4	9	8		3	1	6	
9			7	4	6			3
	2	7				4	9	
3			9	2	1			6
	8	5	2		7	6	3	
1				6				2
		2	4		9	5		

	4	3						1
			7	9	6			
8		7		1			2	5
	1				3	2	6	4
		5	6		7	3		
3	9	6	1				8	
1	8			3		7		6
			2	7	5			
5						4	3	

CROSSWORD

Across

1 WWII leader
5 Spirit in Muslim theology and folklore
11 Potsdam preposition
12 Gomer Pyle player Jim
13 Rigging pro
14 Punish with an arbitrary penalty
15 Cops' way of going on strike: 2 wds.
17 Ecstasy
22 Casual piece of work: 2 wds.
26 Suffix for abnormalities
27 Completely clean
28 "Carrie" director De Palma
29 Mice catchers
30 Game place
31 Whodunit
33 Position on a scale
38 Charles of investment advice
42 Condo
43 Desert: inits., 2 wds.
44 Clinton appointee
45 "L'chaim," literally (Hebrew toast): 2 wds.
46 Brit. awards

Down

1 "Waltz Across Texas" singer Ernest
2 Ancient Greek coin
3 Name in hymns
4 River that flows through Caen, France
5 Forensic site, briefly: 2 wds.
6 Clog: 2 wds.
7 "When Will ___ Loved" (hit for Linda Ronstadt): 2 wds.
8 Scand. land
9 Kristine L. Svinicki's org.
10 Sussex suffix
16 Toad's cousin
18 Ancient neck ornament
19 V.O.A. agency
20 Made out
21 Medieval laborer
22 One-time Tampa Bay Buccaneers tackle Jason
23 ___-eyed
24 Some RBI producers: abbr.
25 And nothing more
28 Welsh word in a Pennsylvania college name
30 Suitable for growing crops
32 ___ Good Feelings: 2 wds.
34 Turkish plateau dweller
35 Chemical suffixes
36 Hombre, once
37 Some Pontiacs, shortly
38 ___ Friday ("Dragnet" role)
39 Bill and ___
40 Jack Black movie "Shallow ___"
41 Major conflict of the 20th century, initially

53

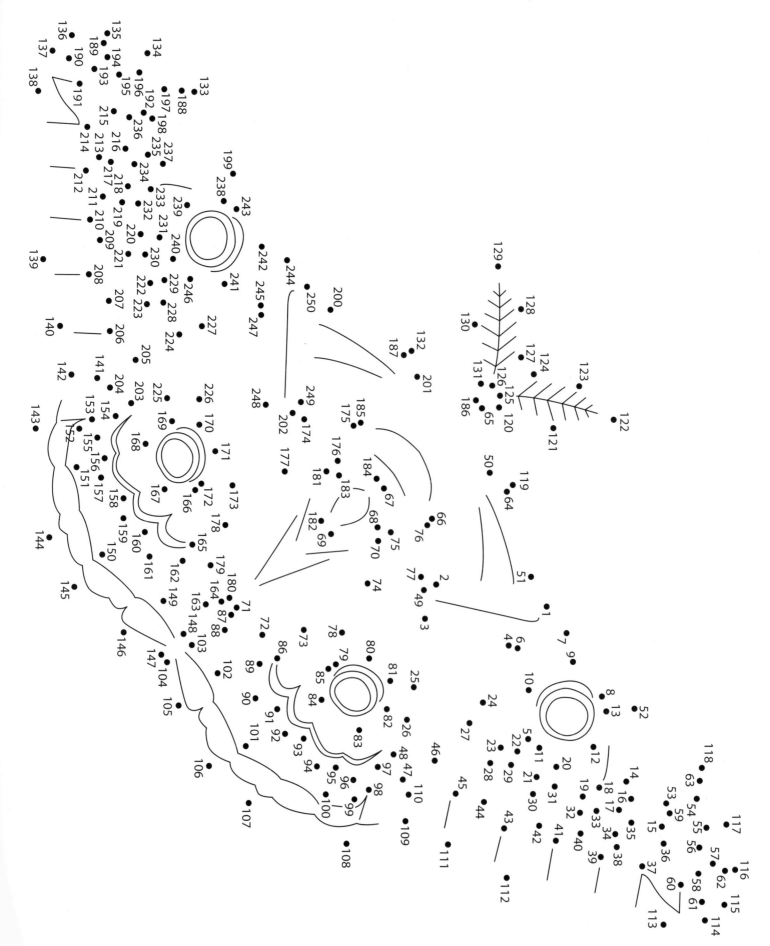

WORD SEARCH
ICE CREAM FLAVORS

```
C O C O N U T J N E W W C O D
H Y R R E B A E T O I O N X I
O Q A Z M N T W B K M I N T J
C N Z T A L O U R R C E T Y H
O N P N N C C U N C E U L R C
L A A I O A I A U A R H Y R T
A B Q F S E R P R F E R S E O
T E F S E T P R I A R P X B C
E E N F P A A T U E M O Y E S
E A F I C U T C H C A E P U R
A O E J L U M C H N K L L L E
T R Y E T A T O B I S C S B T
O G N A M R R Y N F O G A L T
V A N I L L A P N I M F O L U
A L F U D G E B R O W N I E B
```

APRICOT	CHOCOLATE	PISTACHIO
BANANA	COCONUT	PRALINE
BLACKCURRANT	COFFEE	SHERBET
BLUEBERRY	FUDGE	SPUMONI
BUTTERSCOTCH	BROWNIE	TEABERRY
CAPPUCCINO	LEMON	TOFFEE
CARAMEL	MANGO	TUTTI-FRUTTI
CHERRY	PEACH	VANILLA
	PEANUT	

SUDOKU

8			7				4	2
	6	9	2					
	4		5	1		7		8
1					2	8	3	
		6	4		3	5		
	2	8	6					9
4		1		9	7		6	
					5	3	1	
5	3				4			7

		8		9		2		
9		7		4		1		6
	6		5		1		8	
2		9	1		4	8		3
	3		9		2		1	
1		4	6		3	5		9
	9		3		5		7	
7		3		2		6		1
		5		1		3		

CROSSWORD

Across

1 Founded: abbr.
5 It weighs on pilots: 2 wds.
11 Capital of Qatar
12 Spiritual music genre: 2 wds.
13 Historical contest to the death
14 Tiny: var.
15 Natural desire to satisfy hunger
17 Platte River people
18 Swiss watch company
22 Rectifies (a wrong)
24 Wyo. neighbor: 2 wds.
25 Letters for Nittany Lions
26 Dad's namesake: abbr.
27 Artist Nicolaes ___
29 Nickname of 7-Up, with "the"
32 Part of S.S.S.: abbr.
33 Hungarian sheepdog
34 Union
38 Fear
41 Luxurious fabric
42 Skillet coating
43 Snick or ___
44 Make it
45 "What ___!": 2 wds.

Down

1 Icelandic work
2 Cream of mushroom, e.g.
3 Shane MacGowan and bandmates: 2 wds.
4 Letter after gimel: var.
5 Banded metamorphic rock
6 Paws, trotters, etc.
7 Manual's target audience
8 Dormitory heads, for short
9 Special effects used in "Toy Story," e.g.
10 Wide shoe width
16 Youngster
19 Touching, next to
20 Short name for Boone or Webster
21 Gumbo vegetable
22 Dashboard measures, for short
23 "Well, well!": 2 wds.
28 Home for a horse
29 Higher ground
30 Rapa ___
31 Minors' level: 2 wds.
35 Important person
36 "The Alexandria Quartet" finale
37 Gets with great difficulty, with "out"
38 School org.
39 Excited, with "up"
40 Frequently

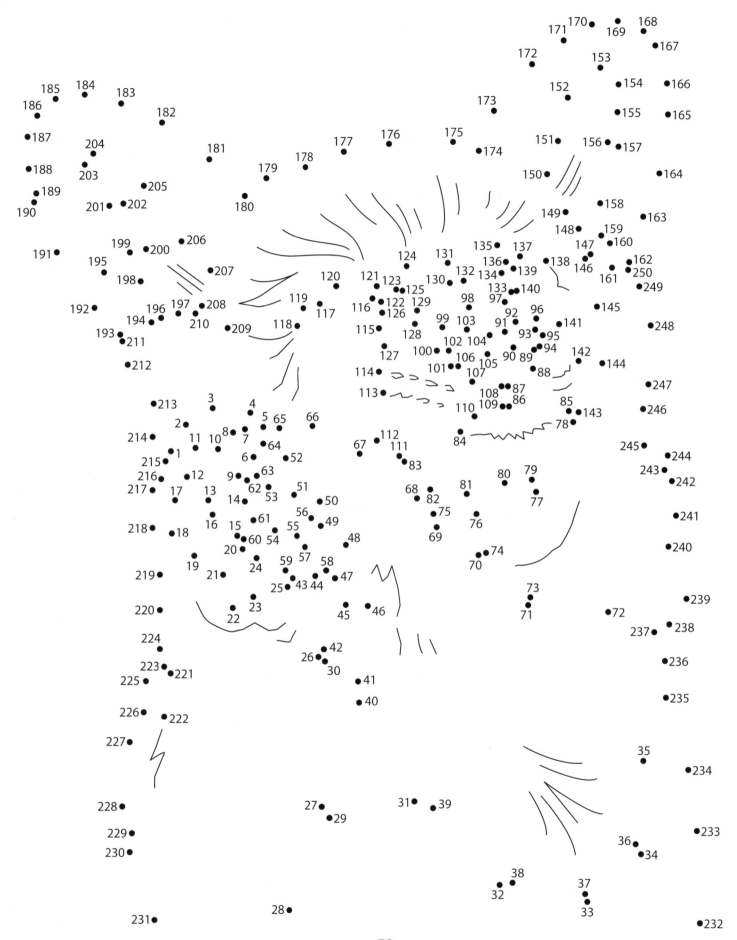

WORD SEARCH
SALAD

```
E O N E O Y Z D E C A R R O T
S T H O U S A N D I S L A N D
I A R P P S F C S A P M A N J
A M E Q T E H R E B M U C U C
N O D S N S C A B L R H J C X
N T P N V W M A L C E E X H F
O N E Q N E A O B L H R H E C
Y L P H T O C T O B O I Y E O
A E P O T A T O E R A T V S L
M T E P E A S U A R H G S E E
E T R R U F Q D O G C S E D S
L U M F U L I C P R L R U X L
H C C A E S A R Y U C H E M A
G E H A H A L U G U R A X S W
O O D A C O V A S F I R F R S
```

ARUGULA	COLESLAW	PEAS
AVOCADO	CROUTON	POTATO
CABBAGE	CUCUMBER	RADISH
CAESAR	FENNEL	RED PEPPER
CARROT	HERBS	SHALLOTS
CELERY	LETTUCE	THOUSAND ISLAND
CHEESE	MAYONNAISE	
CHIVES	MUSHROOMS	TOMATO
		WATERCRESS

SUDOKU

		5	6		1			8
		2	3		8	7		5
1				7			9	
		6	9				8	4
		7		3		1		
2	1				5	3		
	5			2				6
4		1	8		3	9		
9			7		4	5		

8			1	6	5			3
	5		7			1		
3	2		9				7	5
	1		8			2		
4	9						8	6
		6			7		5	
1	3				2		4	9
		8			9		6	
9			5	4	8			7

CROSSWORD

Across

1 Shoot for: 2 wds.
6 German arms manufacturer
11 Angry, old-style
12 Wined and dined
13 Cloth garment
15 Army fatigues, for short
16 Turning points
17 Hoppy glassful, for short
19 Magician's opening
21 Subservient response: 2 wds.
23 College V.I.P.
27 Running wild
29 Letter-shaped opening for a bolt: hyph.
30 Small stream
32 Berlin article
33 Director/producer Kazan
35 Latin foot
36 Puts names to, briefly
39 Hindu titles
41 Skill with which a job is done
45 Grant-___: hyph.
46 Picturesque Ontario gorge town
47 Jeer
48 Was the cause of: 2 wds.

Down

1 Barley bristle
2 Dublin loc.
3 Soft leather shoe
4 One of the Aleutians
5 Subject, to Cicero
6 The Colonel's restaurant
7 Run through
8 Gas, e.g.: abbr.
9 Spa treatment
10 Some printable files, initially
14 Former Virginia senator Charles
17 Month after Nisan
18 Big copper exporter
20 Groove
22 Durable cotton fabric with a velvety nap
24 Careless
25 Rook's spot on a chessboard: 2 wds.
26 Mail carriers have them: abbr.
28 P.D.A. number: abbr.
31 "___ sad sight to see the year dying" (FitzGerald): 2 wds.
34 Synthetic fabric
36 Loretta of "M*A*S*H"
37 Island of the Hudson River
38 German gray
40 Bermuda, e.g.
42 Summer hrs. in Albuquerque
43 "___: Deadliest Roads" (reality TV series)
44 Kung ___ shrimp

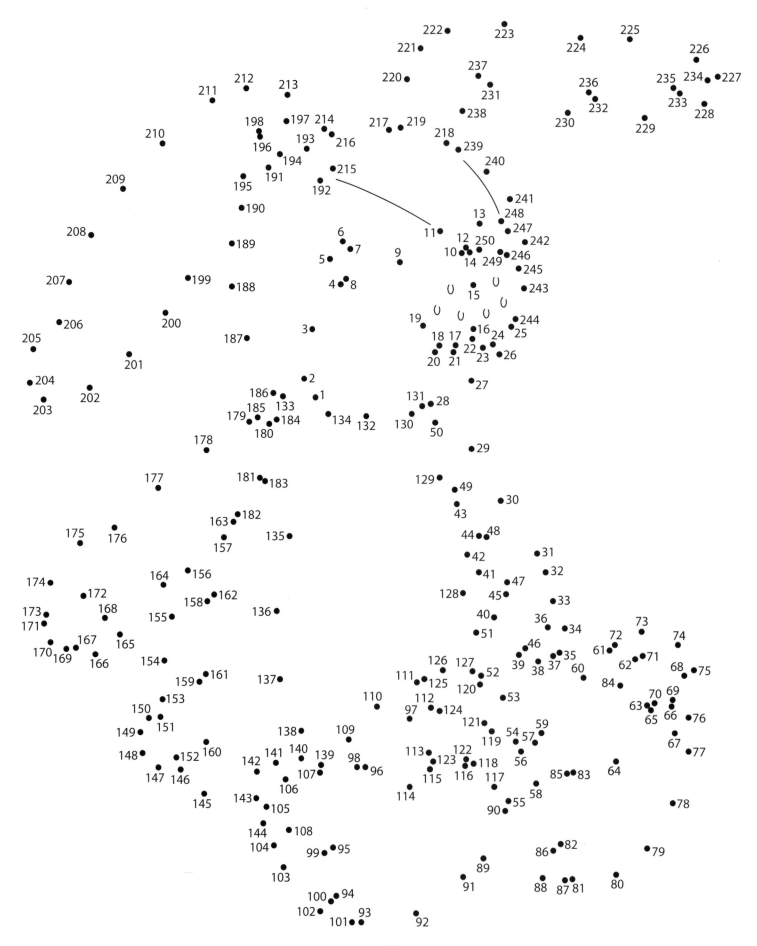

WORD SEARCH
HARVESTTIME

```
C A J V G S A O V S Q U V W S
T O D M M M D B K S U H A T T
H P M I B C B O U T E C U G R
R X W B R K R L P N H N A H A
C B P O I M B V Q E D N R O C
S U P T Q N W E R M F A R P C
P S R J W W E B E Z P O N S I
X C F R T E S Y S T T X O C D
U H B H A Y S T A C K R K B E
A E A V E N Z U A L T R N R R
B R R B H F T R T I F Z E S A
S R L X W R T S N W X T H R A
I I E E R G E G R P E A S A E
L E Y Y N W A K L M R X C E J
O S E W N A A A T E Q J M P M
```

ABUNDANCE	CROPS	PEAS
BARLEY	CURRANTS	PODS
BEET	HAYSTACK	RYE
CARTS	HERBS	SHARE
CHERRIES	HOPS	SILO
CIDER	HUSK	SORTING
COMBINE	NUTS	TRACTOR
CORN	PEARS	WHEAT

SUDOKU

	1		6		4			9
6			8				7	3
5	8		9	1				
		9		6	7	5		
1		5				2		7
		3	1	5		6		
				3	6		1	5
7	3				1			4
4			7		2		8	

	9	4		1		8	6	
7		5		6	8	4		
			2					9
3	8	6			9		7	
	2						1	
	7		3			5	9	6
8					5			
		3	7	9		1		2
	4	7		2		6	3	

CROSSWORD

Across

1 Little whirlpool
5 Blackhawks legend
11 Fifth-century pope who was canonized: 2 wds.
12 Visual
13 Warmonger
14 Keeps from drying out
15 Tavern, old-style
16 Harem chamber
17 Mil. aides
19 Religious figure
23 Sea: Fr.
25 Discontinued: 2 wds.
27 "Out of sight out of mind," e.g.
29 Challenger
30 Supply water
32 Stopping point
33 Crystal ball gazer's phrase: 2 wds.
34 Lang. of Israel
36 English writer Arthur
38 "You've Got a Friend ___" ("Toy Story" tune): 2 wds.
41 Spots on a peacock's tail
44 Place to swim
45 More spacious and well-ventilated
46 JFK takeoff times
47 "Hail the Conquering Hero" actress Ella
48 "Groove Is in the Heart" singers ___-Lite

Down

1 Relating to grades 1-12: hyph.
2 Campus V.I.P.
3 Reduce to a lower level of importance
4 "Yowza!"
5 Sour
6 Like some drinks
7 Iraqi's neighbor
8 ___-de-France
9 Piece of body art, for short
10 Horace's "___ Poetica"
18 Olive-tree genus
20 Temporary insurance certificate: 2 wds.
21 In the blink ___ eye: 2 wds.
22 St. John's island, briefly
23 When doubled, a food fish
24 Brand that has Dibs
26 Unconfined
28 Imaginary and mischievous sprite
31 Taxing org.: 2 wds.
35 Bigfoot, presumably
37 General Robt.: 2 wds.
39 Math calculation
40 Otherwise
41 Pole with a blade on one end
42 Subject of Tom Clancy's "The Good Shepherd"
43 Verdi's "___ tu"

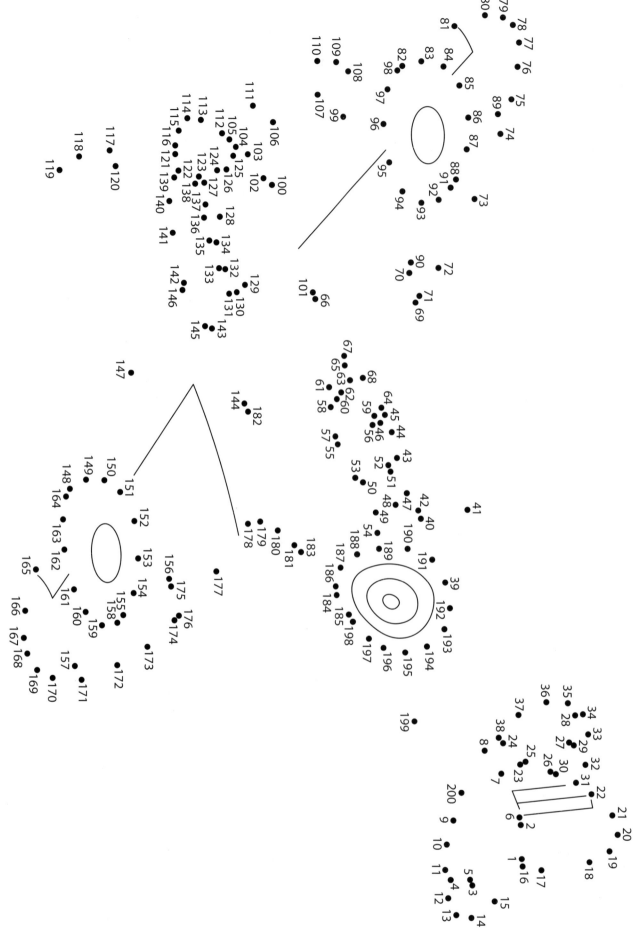

WORD SEARCH
"END" AT THE END

```
D N E L E G E N D T E N D V J
U A S Y I T W E E K E N D L D
N S U S P E N D M W D N E O N
B K P M N U P E N D E Y F C E
E D E D A T T E N D D F Q E D
N N R N D M D E J N E D A N I
D E I E D N T D E N N A P D V
Y C N R E X E M D E N R P W I
F S T P E X M T S U E E R L D
O E E N E O I D N T R V E F Q
R D N N C D O K E O P E H I T
F N D E I G J N E B C R E E R
E O R A E N D E N D U E N N E
N C B E F R I E N D E N D D N
D D N E C S N A R T O D H U D
```

APPREHEND

ATTEND

BEFRIEND

CONDESCEND

CONTEND

DEPEND

DIVIDEND

EXTEND

FIEND

FORFEND

GODSEND

LEGEND

OFFEND

PRETEND

RECOMMEND

REVEREND

SUPERINTEND

SUSPEND

TRANSCEND

TREND

UNBEND

UPEND

WEEKEND

WEND

SUDOKU

4			3		9	1		
		9		2			5	
7			8		1	4		2
3			5			6	1	
2				8				9
	9	7			4			8
9		6	1		8			5
	4			7		3		
		5	2		6			4

		7	6			1	8	
3				5	7		6	
5	8				4	2		
4	1	9		8	5			
	6						3	
			4	2		8	9	1
		8	2				5	6
	9		7	1				2
	7	4			3	9		

CROSSWORD

Across

1 Dining room furniture
6 Replay speed, shortly: hyph.
11 Subway handhold
12 Attend to remaining details: 2 wds.
13 Cheri formerly of "Saturday Night Live"
14 Phrase of explanation: 2 wds.
15 New Deal org.
16 Lustrous fabric
18 From Amsterdam
20 Bowmaking wood
23 Try
25 Radio reporter Raum
26 Make blank
27 Former NBC news anchor Matt
28 Hot
29 Basic monetary unit of Aruba
30 Alphabetic sequence
31 Tether
32 Financial mogul Carl
34 U.S. immigrant's class letters
37 Be brave enough to deal with a problem: 2 wds.
39 As a friend in France: 2 wds.
41 Pipsqueak
42 Like many a TV series
43 Mgrs.' helpers
44 "Get me ___ here!"

Down

1 General ___ Chicken (Chinese menu dish)
2 Firm parts: abbr.
3 Loaf makers: 2 wds.
4 Gibbon of Thailand and Malaysia
5 New Testament letter
6 1969 western starring Glenn Ford
7 City located in San Joaquin County, California
8 1987 #1 hit for Madonna: 3 wds.
9 Greek letters
10 Choose (with "for")
17 Blackjack half
19 "___-daisy!"
21 "… ___ saw Elba": 2 wds.
22 Tip off
23 Peasant worker
24 "To ___ and a bone…" (Kipling): 2 wds.
25 Inner sanctuary of a Greek temple
27 Venezuelan cowboy
29 Jewish word of disapproval
31 Northern Scandinavians
33 Short and to the point
35 Small flake of soot
36 Filmmaker Wertmüller
37 Kingston Trio hit of 1959
38 Jimmy Stewart syllables
40 Modern in Munich

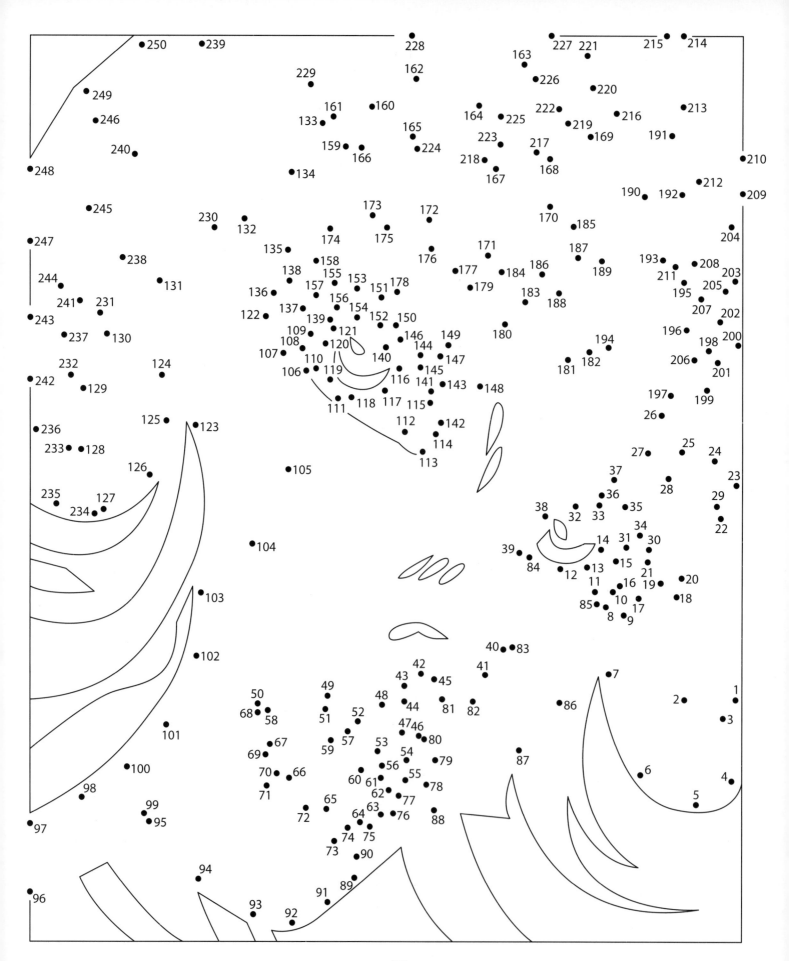

WORD SEARCH
BRISK

```
R B M Y R Y C I M A N Y D G T
T P N Y T R E P R A H S N N R
E G M S N A M I X U P I E C E
N C A T C P G P S L T E N N L
E H G T Z I P P Y A K O L I A
R M I V U D H E R Y N T I M F
G V L C L U D O O O R J V B D
E N E E T W G Y N A P I E L E
T N I Y R I P S M V T B L E T
I O C C V P E S I A O Q Y J I
C A R N A N C Y L F I U R N R
R I I N S R B U S T L I N G I
D D S E I R B E J U B C P V P
M O P D D F I T W D B K B M S
C A A J B R U S Q U E S X Q S
```

ACTIVE

AGILE

ALERT

BRACING

BRUSQUE

BUSTLING

BUSY

CRISP

DYNAMIC

ENERGETIC

HASTY

INVIGORATING

KEEN

LIVELY

NIMBLE

NO-NONSENSE

QUICK

RAPID

SHARP

SMART

SNAPPY

SPIRITED

VITAL

ZIPPY

SUDOKU

3			1			6	8	
	9		4			2		
1				2	6	9		7
5	2			4		1		
	7		6		1		4	
		3		7			9	6
9		5	2	8				3
		8			5		6	
	4	1			9			5

8				6	1	4	9	
1	3						5	
6			8		7			2
	8	3		1	4			
		2	5		8	7		
			7	9		8	6	
2			4		3			5
	9						3	4
	7	4	9	2				6

CROSSWORD

Across

1 Wears away

7 Tangle

10 Neglect

11 Bundle

12 Work boot feature

13 Some addresses, initially

14 "___, I give in!": 2 wds.

15 Throat part

17 Short skirt

18 1930s–40s music hall entertainer Tessie

19 Was present, is now gone

20 Works on bread

21 React to a pun

23 Beginning stage of a study: 2 wds.

26 Order (around)

30 Arterial vessel

31 Acid related to gout

32 Abnormal swellings in the body

34 ___ Park, N.Y.

35 Prefix with graphic

36 Weather phenomenon that means "the boy" in Spanish: 2 wds.

38 Season to be jolly

39 Ready for a drive: 2 wds.

40 Reply: abbr.

41 Thongs

Down

1 Inter

2 New recruit, slangily

3 Soccer score, sometimes: hyph.

4 Old instrument of punishment: 2 wds.

5 That, in Chile

6 Ninth mo.

7 "'night, Mother" playwright Norman

8 Working together

9 Units of magnetic flux density

11 Lab heater: 2 wds.

16 Chaplin, née O'Neill

20 Ornamental carp

22 Bring up

23 Sheen produced by age and polishing

24 Sculptor Jean-Antoine ___

25 Military forces

27 Heinze potato brand: hyph.

28 Enrol: 2 wds.

29 Ice cream spoons

33 Goes down, like the sun

37 Allow

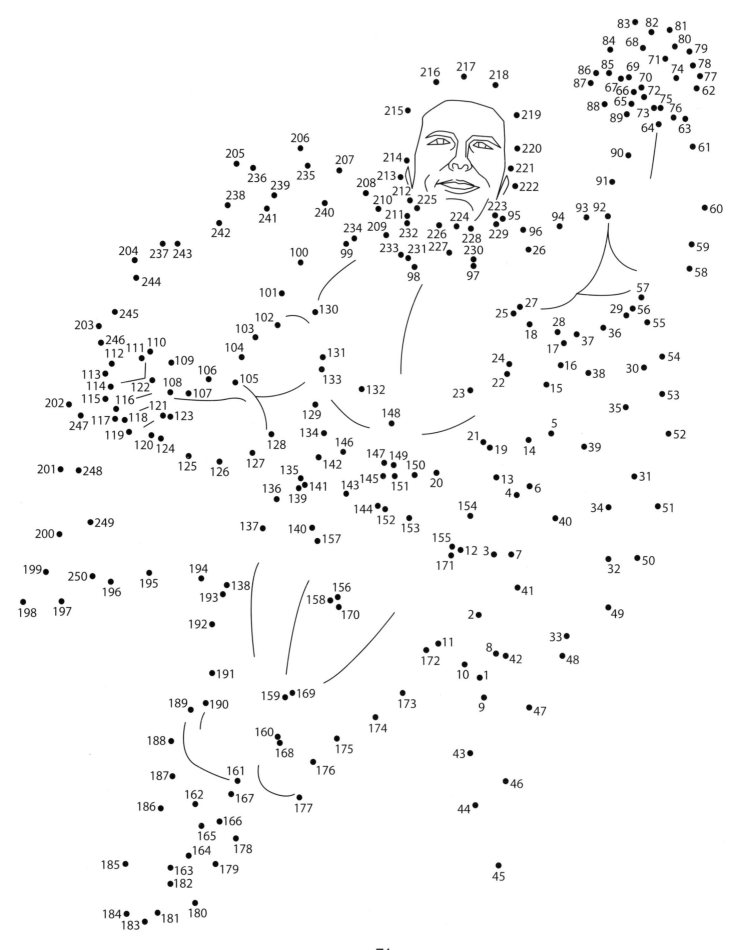

WORD SEARCH
"TIGHT" SPOT

```
H S U Z R T J W L A C E D V K
I U V F E B K S A C Z E A I R
Z X P U N U P L P T Y M X X O
S H I P R P X S Q U E E Z E P
S H T V O X W S V W V R N E E
E W X S C I D H K Y S Z P O N
C E L G I N G N E F W V G K M
U R L I E N I H H A X X H C O
R D N O I T C N U J D S O A G
I Z W T S O G N Y A T B L B C
T K T A N U K R T R U U D R I
Y I E T D S V U E K W D I S U
F T E U K M O T U H X G N I I
X S I I N F C N O U G E G Q R
T U N V D H Q X X G G T B H S
```

AIR	HEAD	SECURITY
BACK	HOLDING	SHIP
BUDGET	HUG	SKIN
CASK	JUNCTION	SQUEEZE
CONTEST	KNIT	STRETCH
CORNER	LACED	TURN
ENDS	MONEY	WAD
FITTING	ROPE	WATER

SUDOKU

	1					3	9	8
7		6			8	5		
4				1	5			
	5			8	4		7	3
1			6		3			9
6	4		7	2			8	
			8	7				4
		5	9			2		6
9	2	4					1	

	4	8						1
			5	7	2			
9		2		1			3	6
	1		8			3	5	4
		6	2		5	8		
8	7	5			1		9	
1	9			8		2		5
			6	2	3			
6						4	8	

CROSSWORD

Across

1 "___, With Love" (Sidney Poitier movie): 2 wds.
6 Canadien, for short
9 Dunne and Ryan
11 Bellow who won the Nobel Prize for Literature in 1976
12 Mismatch: 2 wds.
13 "There ___ time like the present": 2 wds.
14 Suffix with poet or paradox
15 Spanish-language hit song of 1974: 2 wds.
17 Utah ski resort
18 Architectural borders
19 Come across as
20 1985 Pointer Sisters hit: 2 wds.
21 Summit in central Crete: abbr., 2 wds.
23 French "duck"
26 Bothers
30 Make ___ of (mentally highlight): 2 wds.
31 The "E" in Q.E.D.
32 Comes by
34 TV handyman Bob
35 "For ___ be Queen o' the May" (Tennyson): 2 wds.
36 Why
38 Net
39 In profile: hyph.
40 Patty Hearst's kidnap grp.
41 Start of many Latin American place names

Down

1 Shinbones
2 Divine message deliverer
3 Put under
4 Response of body tissues to injury or irritation
5 Sporting goods retailer
6 Bug
7 Fictional character from the Oz books: 2 wds.
8 Woman's upper garment
10 Jeanne d'Arc, e.g.: abbr.
11 Mountain range in southern Spain: 2 wds.
16 Street
20 Pulled off
22 Waste compensation
23 South American rodents
24 Brutish sort
25 Cosa ___, criminal org.
27 Popped up
28 Dunderhead
29 Prefix meaning "tin"
33 Grads-to-be, for short
37 Frozen water, in Frankfurt

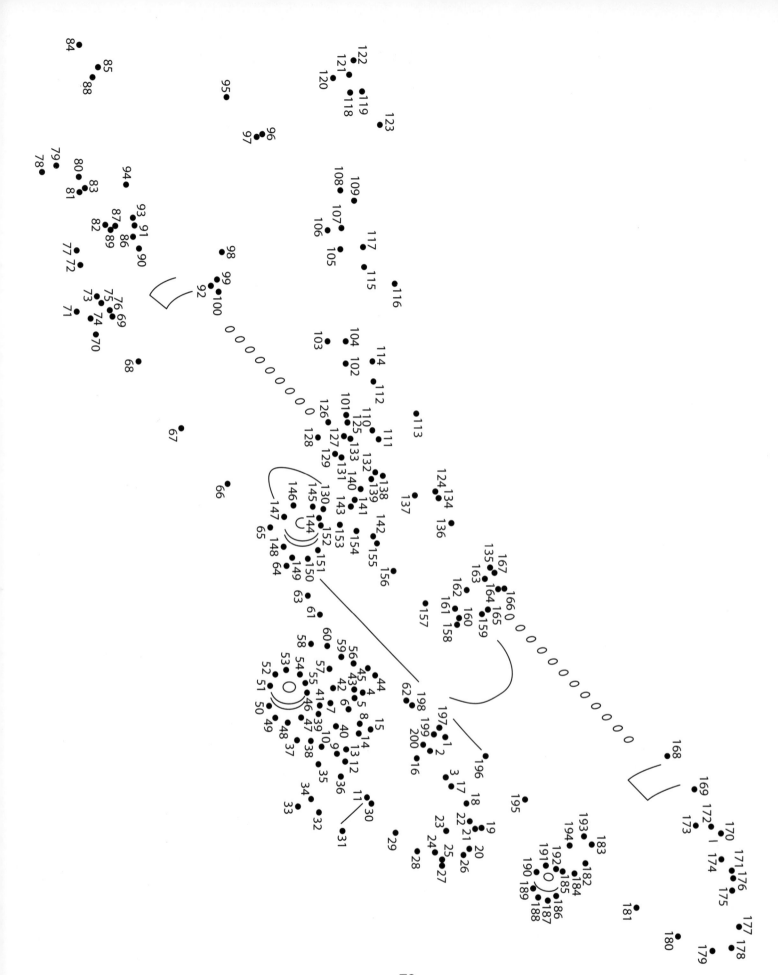

WORD SEARCH
SO TIRED

```
C I S Y J S D Y B Z O Y P T D
I F S L A R P F F D U R O U E
S E Y P A E P A E V I A O O N
F K P I E J X T P R N E P N E
D E N L N N E I L M P W E R K
D E S H E L T G A C U K D O A
D X R U P Y Z U Y N D T E W E
T Z K E S M M E E I E W G H W
A I D W T M Y D D E S Q G H I
E C O I U T V J O N U B A E L
B R M L G R A W U O U C R I T
D E D A J X A H T D K N N K I
A B B U S H E D S E U H U X N
E X H A U S T E D T I U R B G
D E K N O Z T U O D E H S A W
```

BUSHED	JADED	USED UP
DEAD BEAT	PLAYED OUT	WASHED OUT
DEPLETED	POOPED	WEAKENED
DONE IN	RUN RAGGED	WEARY
DRAINED	SAPPED	WHACKED
DROWSY	SHATTERED	WILTING
EXHAUSTED	SLEEPY	WORN OUT
FATIGUED	SPENT	ZONKED

SUDOKU

	4	3					5	2
7		9		2	8			
	1	6		9				3
	8				7	4		
3	6		2		9		1	7
		5	1				6	
4				1		6	9	
			8	5		3		1
5	2					8	7	

7	1					9		3
	2	5		9	4			
6	8			2		1		
4					5		7	
8		1	9		2	5		6
	3		6					8
		7		6			8	2
			4	3		6	1	
9		3					4	5

CROSSWORD

Across

1 "___ the Sheriff" Bob Marley song: 2 wds.

6 Stroke of luck

11 Funny Anne

12 Red ___

13 Manhandle: 2 wds.

14 Domed home

15 Of the stars

17 Delivers a question

18 Gets

20 "Drag Me to Hell" costar Dileep

21 Eds.' requests

24 "Autobahn" group

27 Between: Fr.

28 Poetic contraction

30 Acme

33 Prayer pronoun

36 Group of six

37 Palestinian Islamic movement

39 Very slightly: 2 wds.

40 "Spenser: For Hire" star

41 Giant, bronze automaton given to Europa by Zeus

42 Spendthrift's outing

43 Comic strip dog

Down

1 Damage

2 Japanese delicacy: 2 wds.

3 Thorny shrub or tree

4 "___ Ben Johnson" (inscription on a tomb): 2 wds.

5 Turkic language

6 J. Edgar Hoover ran it, initially

7 Cooking Channel star Emeril

8 WWW addresses

9 Eccentric, slangily

10 Grandson of Eve

16 Hears

19 Showy shooter

22 Able to be upright

23 Archenemy of He-Man

25 Dead: 2 wds.

26 Datebook abbr.

29 Second try at the exam

31 ___-foot oil

32 Rock guitarist, slangily

33 As an example

34 Kind of seal

35 Bahrain ruler

38 "___ Bop" (Cyndi Lauper hit of 1984)

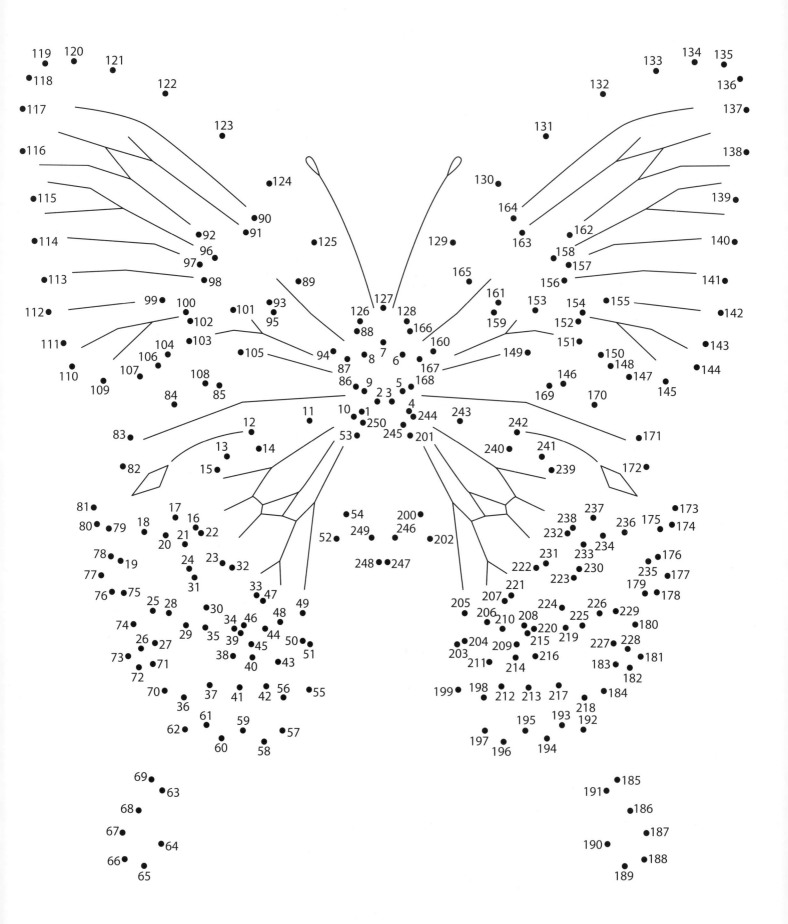

WORD SEARCH
HELP

```
L C H A M P I O N C N K D S F
E W O H N R P F U N D R V H Z
N G R L K E E R E T E C T F K
D D I J L E T T O T S V A A K
A Z G L Z A P R S P R Y G C E
H S J S B U B O A I U V N I V
A N T G E O F O I E N P R L R
N L F R N D A S R L H I I I E
D L O X E I N G I A C P M T S
Z H V K A N X I U D T H E A L
S E E S C D G E H I E E F T C
Q S L Q F A V T D C D W I E U
Q A L R B O B I H X T E I X R
B E N E F I T Y S E Z I S T E
Y G T J B U C U W E N E P E H
```

ABET	FACILITATE	NURSE
ADVISE	FOSTER	OBLIGE
BACK	FUND	PITCH IN
BENEFIT	GUIDE	PROP UP
CHAMPION	HEAL	SERVE
COLLABORATE	HEARTEN	SHORE UP
CURE	LEND A HAND	SIDE WITH
EASE	MINISTER	STRENGTHEN

SUDOKU

	5	7		3		1	9	
1			4		9			6
	6			7			2	
	7	2	9		3	8	6	
8			7		2			9
	3	9	1		8	7	4	
	4			9			8	
7			8		4			5
	8	5		2		9	1	

3	7		4		6		2	8
8			9		7			3
		1		8		6		
		7	3	9	8	4		
2	8						9	5
		4	7	2	5	8		
		9		7		3		
1			8		2			9
7	4		5		9		6	1

CROSSWORD

Across

1 Gives a boost to
6 Petting zoo favorite
11 Zhou ___, prime minister of China 1949–76
12 Hank who hit 755 home runs
13 Grunt
14 Tropical palmlike plant
15 Person staying temporarily in a private home
17 Neptune's scepter
18 52, to Nero
19 Body art
23 "No more for me, thanks": 2 wds.
26 New structuring, as of a business: abbr.
27 Render harmless, in a way
29 Rapper who has feuded with Jay-Z
30 Handout on the street
33 Pipe on a rooftop
36 Not be upfront with: 2 wds.
37 Be wild about
38 "Mirrors 2" star Nick
39 Merchandising gimmick: hyph.
40 Child's response to a taunt: 2 wds.
41 Aegean island

Down

1 Furthur guitarist Phil
2 Very quickly: 3 wds.
3 Thrive
4 Ankle bones
5 Placed
6 Coffered ceiling
7 Outfit (clothing and accessories) for a new baby
8 Rainbows
9 Alternative to a fence
10 "Go on…"
16 Understand
18 Topper
20 Orchestral piece with a rhapsodic theme: 2 wds.
21 Handel's "Messiah," for one
22 Some guys in rap songs, initially
24 Very early, roughly-broken stone implements
25 Vibrating effect
28 A Bobbsey twin
31 Guinness Book listings
32 Actress/model/socialite ___ Hearst-Shaw
33 ___ Field (Mets' ballpark)
34 Part of the body containing the brain
35 Bills with Hamilton on them
36 Powerful hallucinogen, initially

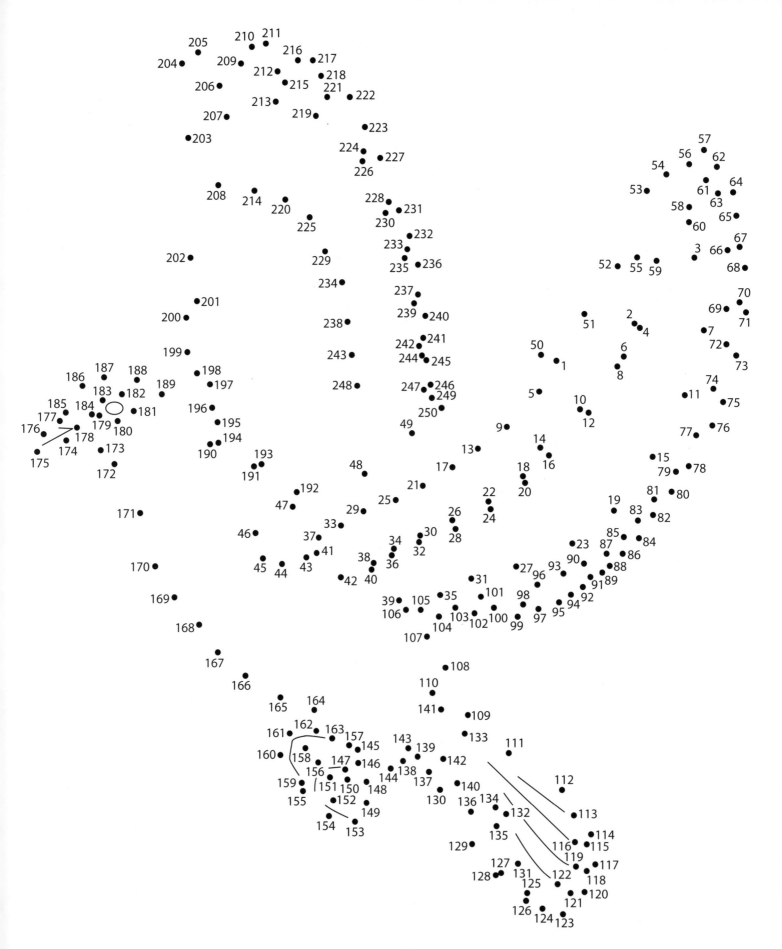

WORD SEARCH
UNDER THE GROUND

```
R E Y Q T O W O R M N B U W L
Y K E M L N F H W V O G H T L
O Z C A U G H H B R E E J C E
L V O A A Y J X E N G D L R W
Z C R I V E R H S T N R W O B
C Z U X Z E O E I E U Y K T M
N T F H G L W N G L D T U R X
K E T R E E G H R L S A K D D
G L R N R H I Z O M E B H T V
J O G R E B K S O O L U A I A
G H L G A M U Z T I F N M U M
G X B D E W E L S J F K G D R
N I A R D D X S B W U E A N X
M U I L E C Y M A S R R M O C
R C B O T A T O P B T C V C P
```

BASEMENT	DUNGEON	RIVER
BOREHOLE	GOLD	ROOTS
BULBS	HADES	SEWER
BUNKER	MAGMA	TRUFFLES
CAVE	MOLE	VAULT
COAL	MYCELIUM	WARREN
CONDUIT	POTATO	WELL
DRAIN	RHIZOME	WORM

SUDOKU

		5	6			2		
4			3	5				9
3	2	8				1	6	5
		3			5			7
	8		2		4		1	
6			9			8		
1	3	7				4	2	8
8				7	1			6
		4			3	9		

					8		6	9
6		8			5	1		
	9	5		4	1			3
		9			2		7	6
	3		5		6		8	
2	7		3			4		
5			8	9		7	1	
		7	1			2		5
3	4		2					

CROSSWORD

Across

1 Actress Jessica and others
6 Prepared to rob, as a house
11 Disputed islands in the East China Sea
12 Lake of talk TV
13 Male sibling with whom one has a parent in common
15 Vintner's prefix
16 Extinguish
17 Anti-Red gp., once
18 Area between Iraq and Kuwait, e.g.: inits.
21 Beyond closing time: hyph.
24 Shut (up)
25 Zeno's home
26 Having wicked thoughts or intentions: hyph.
30 Suffix with arbor or app
31 Medical suffix
32 Baseball's Bud
34 Breathalyzer attachment
37 Jack of diamonds, e.g.: 2 wds.
40 Pitcher's stat.: 2 wds.
41 "Futurama" character with a loopy ponytail
42 Like May through August, letterwise: hyph.
43 Young Jetson

Down

1 "I ___ pleased…": 2 wds.
2 Overdue
3 Bingo call: 2 wds.
4 Small, horned viper
5 Put down by force
6 Squat
7 Islets
8 Timetable
9 Supplement, with "out"
10 Board member: abbr.
14 Outcry
17 Web prog. code
19 Wilbur's horse: 2 wds.
20 Half a Gabor sister's name
21 Thomas ___ Edison
22 Foolproof: hyph.
23 Brit. dictionaries
24 Third section in a dictionary
27 Magical herbs of Greek mythology
28 "The proof of the pudding ___…": 2 wds.
29 Annoy persistently
33 Ogles
34 Heavyweight champ dethroned by Braddock
35 The younger Guthrie
36 Oz greeting
37 Norm
38 "The bad cholesterol," initially
39 Animation frame

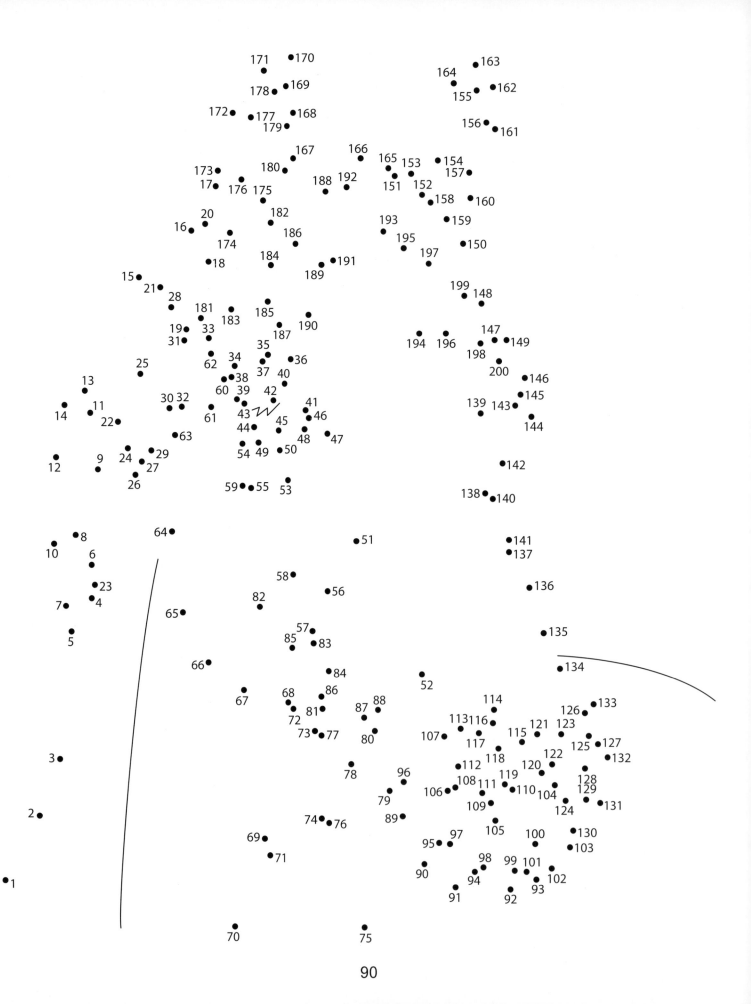

WORD SEARCH
THINGS WITH WINGS

```
I T A M E Y F W Y V E R N D D
B F T I H C C A H P R I Z P J
P I G C W E G D I M B F A Z J
A T H R A Z X C D R I A V U W
T X G O S T R I C H Y T G C D
M A X L P G G R Y P H O N I Q
T O B I D E L G A E O D R J Z
D Q T G R I P F H S F Y G I M
L E O H A R P Y E L A B K O X
S X T T P C X U E V J E S W N
S P A R R O W G C L C Q U O I
K D S W X C N T G R U G S R H
W N R E N A L P A I N O X C P
A O G I Y F D N T A R J X V S
H J J V B B E O T E V X P E F
```

ANGEL	FAIRY	MOSQUITO
BAT	GNAT	MOTH
BIRDS	GOOSE	OSTRICH
CRANE	GRYPHON	PLANE
CROW	HARPY	SPARROW
CUPID	HAWK	SPHINX
EAGLE	MICROLIGHT	WASP
EROS	MIDGE	WYVERN

SUDOKU

6		2			8	9		1
		9	2	3	4	7		
	4				6			2
	1				7			4
7		3				5		8
2			6				3	
3			8				7	
		6	7	5	2	8		
5		8	1			4		9

8			1			6	9	
	4		3			2		
1				2	6	4		7
5	2			3		1		
	7		6		1		3	
		8		7			4	6
4		5	2	9				8
		9			5		6	
	3	1			4			5

CROSSWORD

Across

1 Become boring
5 Shortly: 3 wds.
11 Shoe brand
12 Adams' predecessor
13 Musical equipment company
14 Capital of Kazakhstan
15 Catching (as a disease)
17 Demanding
18 "In ___ and out the other": 2 wds.
21 Recently: abbr.
25 Theology sch.
26 Neighbor of Den. and Fin.
27 Israeli guns
29 Fruit-eating bird with a huge bill
32 Pulls with effort
34 Scooby-Doo and others: 2 wds.
39 Small trinket
40 Like some truth
41 Busy
42 Musical notes
43 Numbers games
44 Words before "of false teeth" or "of tennis": 2 wds.

Down

1 Jardin Atlantique, par exemple
2 Chevrolet subcompact car
3 Describe
4 Chinese philosopher: hyph.
5 Graphics machine
6 Adamant refusal: 2 wds.
7 Cleopatra's love
8 Brew, in Germany
9 Plasma particles
10 Contents of some bags

16 ___ glance (quickly): 2 wds.
18 The Buckeyes, briefly
19 ___ Perce (Native Americans)
20 British record label letters, once
22 Bailout key
23 Windhoek's land, once: inits.
24 Perfect rating
28 Month before Adar
29 Private pupils
30 No spring chicken

31 Patriotic chant: 2 wds.
33 Finnish architect Alvar ___
34 Football kicker Yepremian
35 Peewee
36 Gps. like Rockefeller Foundation and Save the Children, to the UN
37 Glamour rival
38 Way: abbr.
39 Arg. neighbor

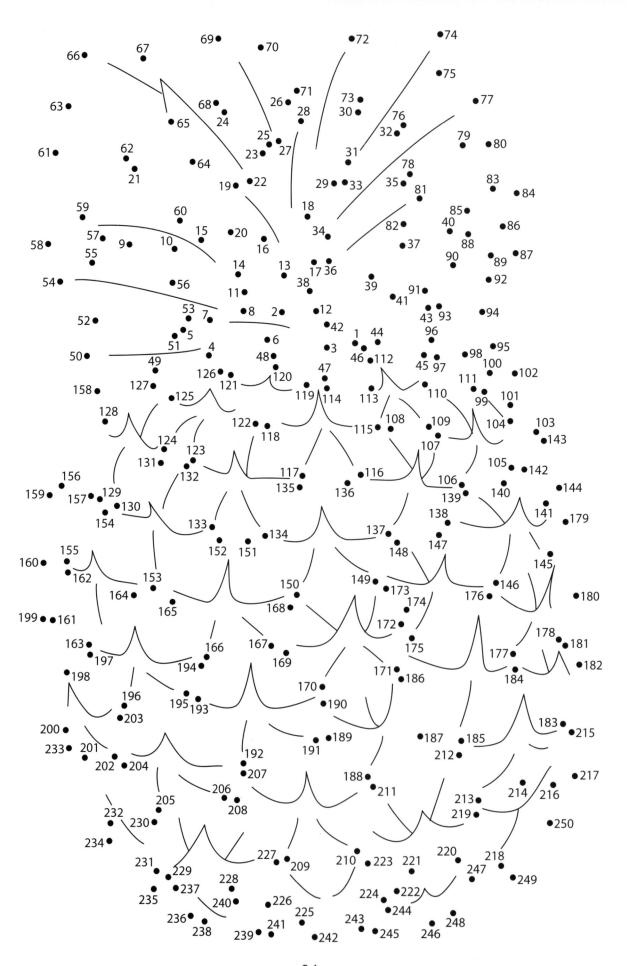

WORD SEARCH
SIGNS

```
P N O S I O P T B T T W N P L
M O N E U I U U O I A H W G O
S F T R B N M O N E W A Y D O
I T L S L P O S W W L N S T H
G B A L S T Z I Z K O T E G C
B K H I T U N J T U W S K G S
F S A E R U B I T U A C N F E
R M E K L S R U A E A I G I L
W E R I C P R N L P L C I R C
U A G D C N W P R C T F J E I
S N R N Y N T A Y I L E C E H
L W S N A E A C N O G I W X E
O X D A I D O C O T L H W I V
W J Y U F N Z D A O E I T T O
Q J Q I X E G S P V Q D S S N
```

BUMPS	NO CYCLING	SLOW
BUS STOP	NO U-TURN	STAIRS
CAUTION	NO VEHICLES	TURN RIGHT
DANGER	ONE WAY	UNSAFE
FIRE EXIT	POISON	VACANCIES
FLOOD	POLICE	WALK
HALT	QUIET PLEASE	WARNING
HELP WANTED	SCHOOL	WET PAINT

SUDOKU

	3	5	1	6			4	
4					3	8	7	
				4				5
	2	1	8			6	9	
6				2				3
	9	4			5	7	2	
8			9					
	5	9	7					1
	6			4	2	5	8	

	4	3		2				7
	5	7					1	6
8		2		6	9			
	9				8	5		
7	3		6		2		4	8
		1	4				3	
			9	1		7		4
1	6					9	8	
5				4		3	2	

CROSSWORD

Across

1 "I don't wanna hear it!," initially
4 Staff
7 New Testament book: abbr.
8 Jim Bakker's club letters
11 Sabotage carried out for ecological reasons
13 Golfing great ___ Trevino
14 Palindromic Preminger
15 A-12 ___, supersonic reconnaissance plane
17 Trumpet effect: hyph.
19 Maltese money, once
20 Fed. support benefit
21 "This is serious!": 3 wds.
23 Hide-hair connector
25 Cobb of baseball fame et al.
26 Increase
29 Buddy
32 "Hawaii Five-0" nickname
33 Writer Welty
35 Early game score: hyph.
37 D.D.E. namesakes
38 1960s protest grp.
39 Most tense or nervous
41 Cologne cooler
42 Itinerary abbr.
43 #s
44 In one's interest

Down

1 "___ Carter" (Lil Wayne album)
2 Unit of electrical resistance
3 Wild goat of the Pyrenees
4 Cat calls
5 Take the role of: 2 wds.
6 Oblivion
8 Frank: hyph.
9 Wife of the late Steve Irwin, a.k.a. "The Crocodile Hunter"
10 "The state," to King Louis XIV
12 Service station offering
16 Henry or Cassius
18 Frigid or million ending
22 Words to Brutus: 2 wds.
24 "Typee" sequel
26 "___ of Rock 'n' Roll" (Ringo Starr hit of 1976): 2 wds.
27 Nicholson Baker story: 3 wds.
28 Must: 2 wds.
30 "You ___ Beautiful" (Cocker hit of 1975): 2 wds.
31 Goes on and on
34 502, in Herod's day
36 Vortex Mini Ultra Grip Football manufacturer
40 Merkel's nat.

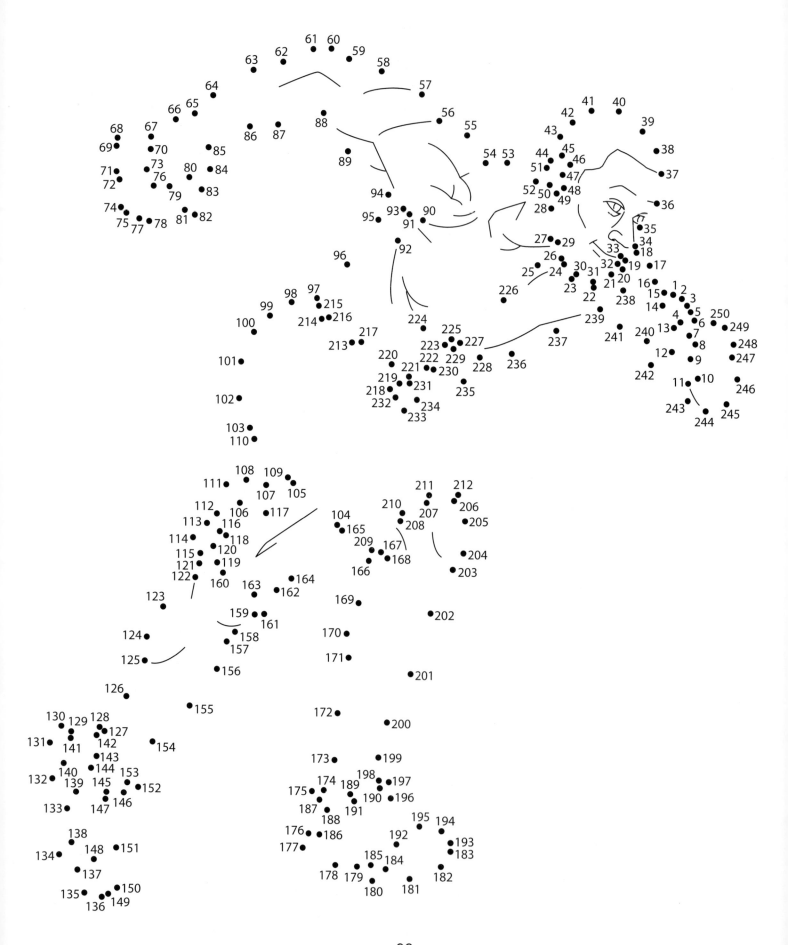

98

WORD SEARCH
FABRICS

```
Z N J M E Z N E J S A J E Z Q
Z I O X P W Y G L E A T H E R
F T I R A G G K V S N N J F O
K A L L G X R A S A I O T N N
I S S D A A O P I E N L I Y M
U H K O Y A N S D N Y R L M Z
N C I O B T S Z D I E O M G T
S A N C N E H X A M N K A F N
I N T E H F I W T R T S H N I
L V Q R T F L I N E N N G S H
L A B P A A E C Q F G E N E C
A S C F B T B Y D N C R I R S
H V P E K L D U D W F I G G W
C K F O R E T S E Y L O P E X
T K E D E U S F R E T M W U N
```

CANVAS	LEATHER	ORLON
CHALLIS	LINEN	POLYESTER
CHINTZ	LISLE	RAYON
ERMINE	MERINO	SATIN
GINGHAM	MOIRE	SERGE
HESSIAN	NYLON	SUEDE
LACE	OILSKIN	TAFFETA
LAWN	ORGANZA	TARTAN

SUDOKU

6								7
	4			3			9	
		8	6		7	4		
8	3		2		9		7	5
			3		8			
2	9		7		1		8	6
		1	9		6	5		
	8			2			1	
5								3

		5		7		2	6	9
		3		1	6			
		8	9					
8							5	
	2	9				4	1	
	6							7
					5	7		
			6	4		3		
4	5	2		8		6		

CROSSWORD

Across

1 Of the country
6 Prevailing weather
11 Years old: 2 wds.
12 "Stay of Execution" author Stewart
13 "Green Acres" actor: 2 wds.
15 Pirates' pelf
16 Drugstore chain
17 Suffix for assist or resist
19 Prefix with pressure
22 Playground retort: 3 wds.
25 Genesis man
26 Philosophical doctrine (the converse of free will)
28 Piecrust ingredient
29 Outdoor meal
30 Time-line span
31 Actor Oka of "Heroes"
32 Tore
33 Modern info holders, initially
37 Communication device with a dial: 2 wds.
41 Skeleton part
42 Romero of the screen
43 Viewpoint
44 Nonpoetic writing

Down

1 100 sen in Cambodia
2 Destroy
3 James who co-wrote "Hair"
4 Disturbed, charged up
5 Civil War general
6 Produce a young cow
7 Canadian law degrees, initially
8 Ending for prom or prem
9 Acidic humus
10 FRER competitor
14 Escort
18 "...___ a lender be"
19 Has ___ with (is connected): 2 wds.
20 So, in Sorrento
21 "Jarheads" org.
22 Not doing anything productive
23 Tootsie
24 ___ vez (again, in Spain)
25 Put into code
27 "___ for insect": 2 wds.
31 Russian tennis player, ___ Safin
32 Game delayer
34 "Take care of it": 2 wds.
35 Miscellanies (suffix)
36 Without moisture
37 Some N.F.L.ers
38 Sesame, olive or canola
39 As yet unscheduled: inits.
40 Animal tranquilizing drug, initially

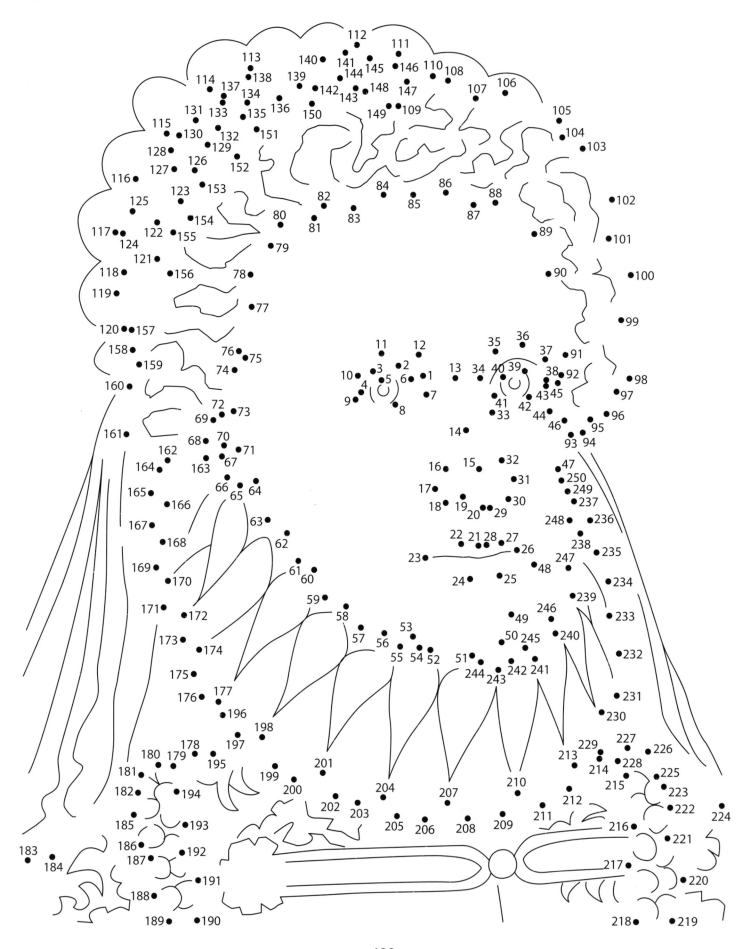

WORD SEARCH
WAKE UP

```
N P U C A E T S U N R I S E F
T Y S G T O J L O A S F H Z L
O V T N A S S I O R C F O O A
O V E R S L E P T H E S W O N
T V M W E M B P B S O Y E N N
H F U A S A J E I H C N R S E
B Z E S I Q A R C O T H K G L
R Y S H C R A S F S A A N N L
U A L I R X R F A I E I I A S
S W I N E H E F R R S B E Z C
H N Z G X E K B B S D R E D R
P I B L E A R Y E Y E D L Y A
G N Z C E U A R O C M K O A T
U G V R S D D Q N E K A W A C
G K B H C O C K C R O W R F H
```

ARISE	DAYBREAK	SHOWER
AWAKEN	DRESSING	SLIPPERS
BLEARY-EYED	EXERCISES	SNOOZE
BREAKFAST	FLANNEL	SUNRISE
CEREAL	HAIRBRUSH	TEACUP
COCK-CROW	MUESLI	TOOTHBRUSH
COFFEE	OVERSLEPT	WASHING
CROISSANT	SCRATCH	YAWNING

SUDOKU

		9		2		4	5	7
		1	5					
		3		6	7			
	1							9
4		5				8		6
7							2	
			7	8		3		
					9	2		
9	8	4		1		7		

	8			3			9	
9			1		4			6
		5	7		2	3		
2	9						4	1
		1				5		
5	7						3	8
		3	6		1	9		
4			9		3			5
	2			7			6	

CROSSWORD

Across

1 Female fortune-teller
6 Captain Hook's bo'sun
10 Young child's word for a cow: 2 wds.
12 It grows on trees
13 Shoeless
14 ___ Loma, Calif.
15 ___ Raymonde, player of Alex Rousseau on "Lost"
17 Fighting Tigers' home, briefly
18 Mo preceder
20 Scrumptious, to a child
22 "___ money" (college student's request)
24 One millionth of a meter
27 Lively ballroom dance
29 100 kobo in Nigeria
30 "___ No Place Like Home" ("The Wizard of Oz" quote)
32 Blows up, initially
33 Universal donor: 2 wds.
35 Clock std.
36 Meal starter
38 Arm bender
40 New, to Otto
42 Illness
45 Chief
46 2001 French film starring Audrey Tautou
47 Opposing votes
48 Griffith and Williams

Down

1 The Mustangs of the N.C.A.A.
2 Ca+, K+ or Na+
3 Salad ingredient: 2 wds.
4 Jewish youth org.
5 Crackers
6 Little, in Leith
7 "Pretty in Pink" star: 2 wds.
8 Guesses: abbr.
9 Levi's uncle
11 Ill will
16 Former Ugandan tyrant
18 E-5 in the U.S.A.F.
19 Mrs. Rabin
21 Future doc's exam
23 Flat-bottomed boat
25 Biscuit bits
26 Lampooner of Tweed
28 ___ Le Pew, French skunk
31 1965 march site
34 The 44th president
36 Second son of Judah
37 Sleek, briefly
39 Pulitzer-winning author Robert ___ Butler
41 Hesitant sounds
43 Home improvement letters
44 Positive reply

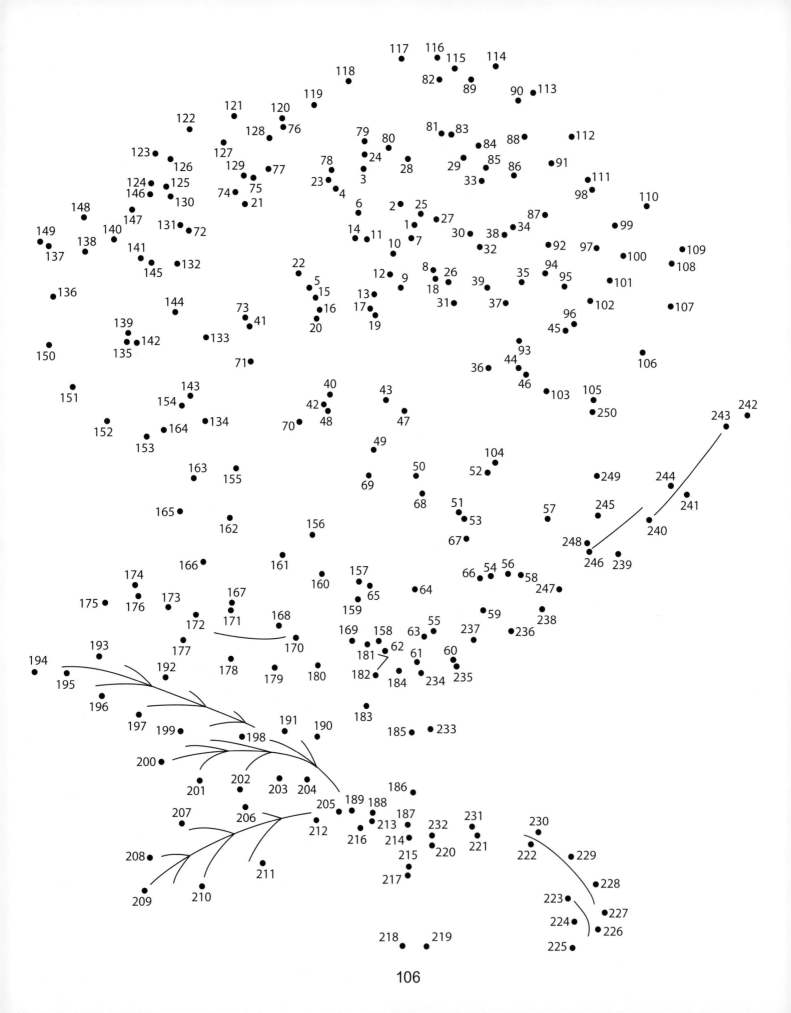

WORD SEARCH
WIND AND BRASS INSTRUMENTS

```
B A S S T U B A G P I P E S G
M E L O D I C A A N I R A C O
F S N E L T S I H W N I T O F
N N P O D U S E V A N Y L C N
E A R L B L K B A S S O O N R
K A Z O O M U P R A O R N E O
Y H T J H G O C I U N R D P H
R O R E L H O R F E O R O I L
A R B E P D C F T H O A V C E
F N M T Q M L N T C D S I C G
O P S F U U U E E B O A U O U
H I H N T A S R F R W B F L L
S P A E J S H S T I F H O O F
R E W O A B C A C O F Q G E M
R O M B R D I D G E R I D O O
```

BAGPIPES	FLUGELHORN	OCARINA
BASS TUBA	FLUTE	PICCOLO
BASSET HORN	FRENCH HORN	RECORDER
BASSOON	HAUTBOY	SHAWM
BUGLE	HORNPIPE	SHOFAR
CORNET	KAZOO	TIN WHISTLE
DIDGERIDOO	MELODICA	TROMBONE
FIFE	OBOE	TRUMPET

SUDOKU

3			9		6			7
	4						6	
5	7						1	4
		4	1	2	8	6		
		9	7	3	5	2		
4	9						3	1
	5						2	
6			8		4			9

	4	1	9		6	7	8	
	8						3	
			7	8	4			
	5	2	1		9	4	7	
		4				9		
	7	9	8		5	2	1	
			2	9	1			
	1						6	
	9	8	6		3	1	2	

CROSSWORD

Across

1 ___ dawn: 2 wds.
5 ___ couture
10 Sides of a pie slice, geometrically
12 Building addition
13 Swimming moves
15 One, in France
16 Preceded
17 It may be added to port or pot
18 X, Y, or Z, e.g.: abbr.
19 The Matterhorn for one
20 Carrier to Karachi
21 Org.
23 Sheen
25 Shaped like Humpty Dumpty
27 Rumormonger
30 Atkins no-no, briefly
34 Get on in years
35 Genealogically-based community service organization, initially
37 Corp. bigwig
38 Grammar school basics, for short
39 Wine grade
40 Part of "C in C": abbr.
41 Polygraph: 2 wds.
44 Atlanta Open winner in 2013, 2014, 2015, 2017, and 2018
45 Claim of ignorance, slangily
46 "I Feel For You" singer Khan
47 Theater magnate Marcus

Down

1 "Rocannon's World" author Le Guin
2 Describes in vivid detail
3 Some snakes
4 Make fast
5 At a loss: 2 wds.
6 "It's ___-win situation": 2 wds.
7 Discarded
8 Sixteenth of a dollar, slangily
9 Movie has-been: hyph.
11 Island in Spain
14 Discern the difference between: 2 wds.
22 Dissenting votes
24 "Hold on a ___!": abbr.
26 Guts
27 Vampire repellent
28 Like a man-eating giant
29 Tennis champion ___ Williams
31 Bank customer's ID: abbr., 2 wds.
32 Fixed
33 Have on loan
36 Like many a mistake
42 Prefix meaning "ten": var.
43 ___-de-sac (blind alley)

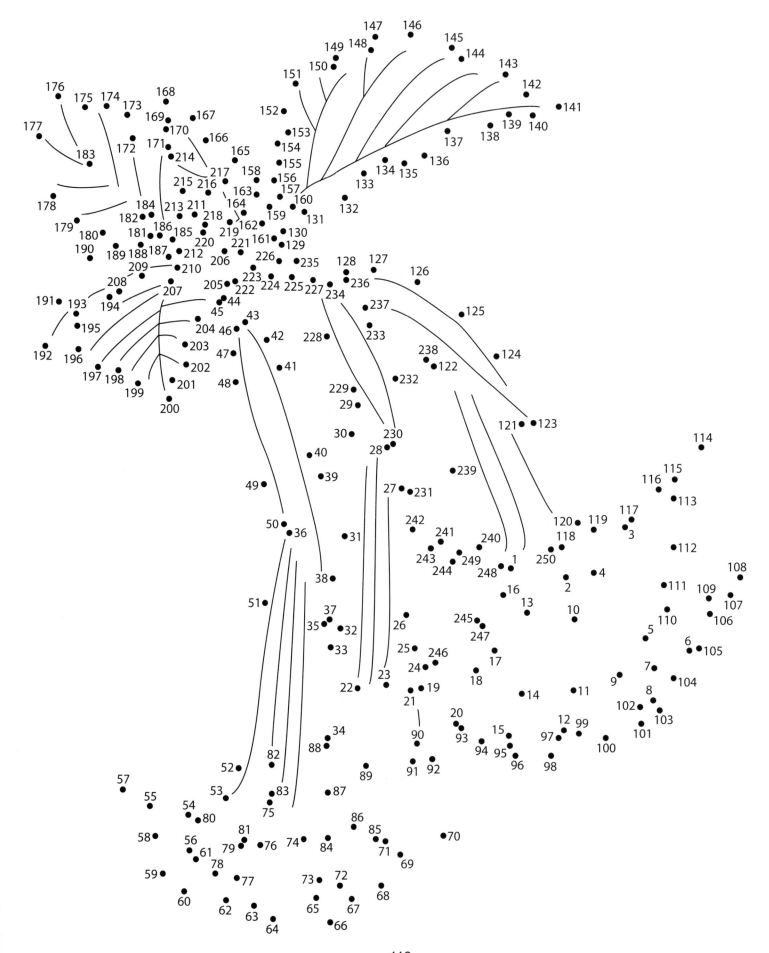

WORD SEARCH
THINGS THAT FLOW

```
N P Y X J H U D L O R T E P M
B M E N I L O S A G N T L V P
A G B S H H Q V R E I B K Y G
W N Y A P E T M R D A O C B Q
I I E L P P I R E C M S I M F
W S M I H Q U S K U G Z R A N
L S R V G C W W T W A M T E I
T E L A R A A W U R M V A T F
A R Q I V S I T I B E E Z S F
L D A E H G F O U N T A I N A
E D S F C T O J M J E O M V R
D A H R F G A E V K F E A U A
D L E E C I U J P Q L L K J P
Y A B E E R C S L I B I H J D
M S T Z J R A G R A V Y M N T
```

AIR CURRENT	JUICE	SALIVA
BACKWASH	LAVA	STEAM
BEER	MAGMA	STREAM
CREAM	MILK	TIDES
EDDY	PARAFFIN	TRAFFIC
FOUNTAIN	PETROL	TRICKLE
GASOLINE	RIPPLE	WAVES
GRAVY	SALAD DRESSING	WINE

111

SUDOKU

5			3		4			6
		4				3		
9		6		8		1		7
			8		9			
		1				4		
			1		5			
3		8		5		2		1
		2				9		
6			2		1			8

					3			1
		2				6		
		7	4	6		3		
				2		7	8	
	2	9	6		8	1	5	
	5	4		1				
		6		3	4	9		
		5				8		
4			2					

CROSSWORD

Across

1 Journalist Joseph
6 Pierre Corneille play: 2 wds.
11 Boito's Mefistofele, e.g.
12 Massey of old movies
13 Die, slangily: 3 wds.
15 ICU staffers
16 Hemingway's "The Old Man and the ___"
17 Go-___ (1980s band)
18 Straw roof
20 Big name in toilet cleaners: hyph.
23 Suffix with million
26 Rival of both Clinton and Bush
27 ___ the Jebusite (Biblical figure who sold his threshing floor to David)
28 "Nana" star Anna
29 Helios, for example: 2 wds.
30 Fill with bubbles
32 Tally (up)
34 Crude liquid
35 Tai leader
38 He had a traveling Wild West Show: 2 wds.
41 Draconian
42 1972 Bill Withers hit: 2 wds.
43 Parceled (out)
44 Carvey and Rohrabacher

Down

1 Shortened form, for short
2 Rested
3 Concordes, e.g.
4 Chemistry suffix
5 Firearm missile aimed at an easy or casual target
6 "___ my mercy all my enemies" ("The Tempest"): 2 wds.
7 "The March" author's monogram
8 Showing symptoms of a cold
9 Words before "doing": 2 wds.
10 Some cassettes, briefly
14 Make well
18 Dog treat: hyph.
19 Meat, on a cantina menu
20 Defaces with rolls?: abbr.
21 Up to now
22 Appalling
24 Indian P.M., 1991–6
25 Last stop
27 Audibly: 2 wds.
29 Spinnaker, e.g.
31 Chemistry Nobelist Hoffmann
32 Alphabet starters
33 Old Spanish coin
35 Carriage
36 Mrs. Alfred Hitchcock
37 French islands
39 Service charge
40 Troop grp.

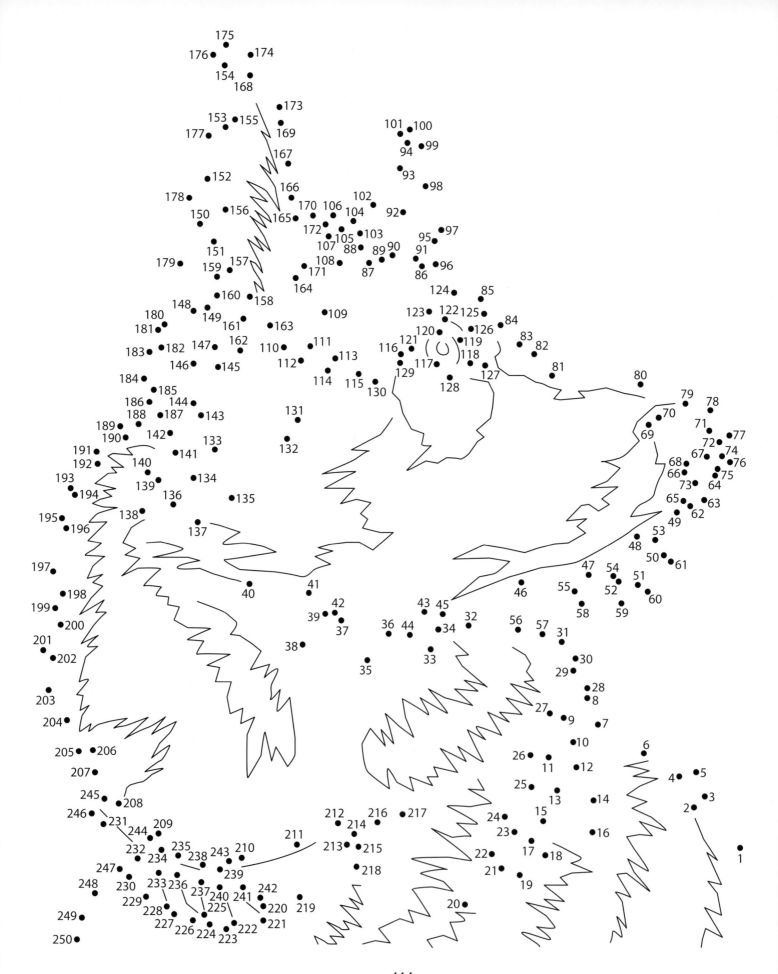

WORD SEARCH
MADE OF PAPER

```
M M I R O R A D N E L A C L Y
B B D X K S Z C O E W C J E Y
R A X R E Q D I N C N E N B L
E Q G T D C H I H U U O W A D
P Z A S F G Z V D S M M Z L A
A L B M K A W C S M E R E K P
P N W Z G I Q I I U N E M N E
L A E A N P T A N D X P X B T
L P M C Z R V E I G N P G P O
A K Q P D Z F O M Y A A N A N
W I L I H B I L L R B R O M X
G N A T J L H U A A P W P N N
O R R N E S E S E Y O C U N Y
Y K C A S X O T A N B B O O K
I Z T S E L R E W O L F C M N
```

BAGS	KITE	PAMPHLET
BILL	LABEL	PARASOL
BOOK	MAGAZINE	PLATES
CALENDAR	MAP	SACK
COUPON	MENU	TEA BAG
DIARY	MONEY	TISSUE
DOCUMENT	NAPKIN	WALLPAPER
FLOWER	NOTEPAD	WRAPPER

SUDOKU

<table>
<tr><td></td><td></td><td>7</td><td></td><td>2</td><td></td><td></td><td>9</td><td></td></tr>
<tr><td>5</td><td></td><td></td><td></td><td></td><td>3</td><td>6</td><td>4</td><td></td></tr>
<tr><td>3</td><td>4</td><td></td><td></td><td></td><td></td><td></td><td></td><td>8</td></tr>
<tr><td>1</td><td></td><td>4</td><td></td><td></td><td>2</td><td></td><td></td><td></td></tr>
<tr><td></td><td></td><td></td><td></td><td></td><td></td><td></td><td></td><td></td></tr>
<tr><td></td><td></td><td></td><td>1</td><td></td><td></td><td>5</td><td></td><td>7</td></tr>
<tr><td>4</td><td></td><td></td><td></td><td></td><td></td><td></td><td>7</td><td>3</td></tr>
<tr><td></td><td>8</td><td>1</td><td>5</td><td></td><td></td><td></td><td></td><td>6</td></tr>
<tr><td></td><td>9</td><td></td><td></td><td>6</td><td></td><td>1</td><td></td><td></td></tr>
</table>

<table>
<tr><td>6</td><td></td><td></td><td>8</td><td></td><td></td><td></td><td>9</td><td></td></tr>
<tr><td></td><td>9</td><td>3</td><td>5</td><td></td><td></td><td>7</td><td></td><td></td></tr>
<tr><td></td><td></td><td>5</td><td></td><td></td><td></td><td></td><td>1</td><td>4</td></tr>
<tr><td></td><td></td><td></td><td></td><td></td><td>2</td><td></td><td>3</td><td></td></tr>
<tr><td>9</td><td></td><td></td><td></td><td></td><td></td><td></td><td></td><td>2</td></tr>
<tr><td></td><td>8</td><td></td><td>6</td><td></td><td></td><td></td><td></td><td></td></tr>
<tr><td>4</td><td>7</td><td></td><td></td><td></td><td></td><td>1</td><td></td><td></td></tr>
<tr><td></td><td></td><td>1</td><td></td><td></td><td>6</td><td>3</td><td>8</td><td></td></tr>
<tr><td></td><td>6</td><td></td><td></td><td></td><td>1</td><td></td><td></td><td>5</td></tr>
</table>

CROSSWORD

Across

1 Behind bars
6 Cram
10 Swelling shrinker: 2 wds.
12 College head, slangily
13 Artist who painted "The Judgment of Paris"
14 Perseverance motto starter: 2 wds.
15 Enroll in the army
17 Music from Jamaica
19 Singer Sumac
20 Trendy
23 Person in the news, briefly
25 Circumspect
27 Love, Italian-style
28 Russian Revolution leader
29 ___ Carta
30 ___ Linda, city southeast of Los Angeles
31 Work steadily at
32 Lady in personal ads, initially
34 "Am ___ your way?": 2 wds.
35 Good-for-nothing
37 Vestments, e.g.
40 Blue ___, sea cave of Capri
43 Pedestal part
44 Sew together
45 Mobutu ___ Seko of Zaire
46 Lots

Down

1 Geometric fig.
2 Adept
3 History of the descent of families
4 Dark, in poems
5 Online magazine named for a fictional newspaper in an Evelyn Waugh novel (with "The"): 2 wds.
6 Polish's partner
7 It may come from a pound
8 Caffeine source
9 Business card info.
11 Not very funny
16 Strike out: 2 wds.
17 Rapscallion
18 ___ Pasha, Turkey's Atatürk
20 "The Stars Fell on ___" (Robert Duvall movie of 1995)
21 African antelope
22 1979 Alda senatorial role
24 Ending for east or west
26 Fair hiring letters, for short
33 Fake hairpieces
35 Woodwind lower than a piccolo
36 French silk
37 Dept. store merchandise
38 Dental org.
39 Country rtes.
41 ___/IP (Internet connection standard)
42 Raised-eyebrow remarks

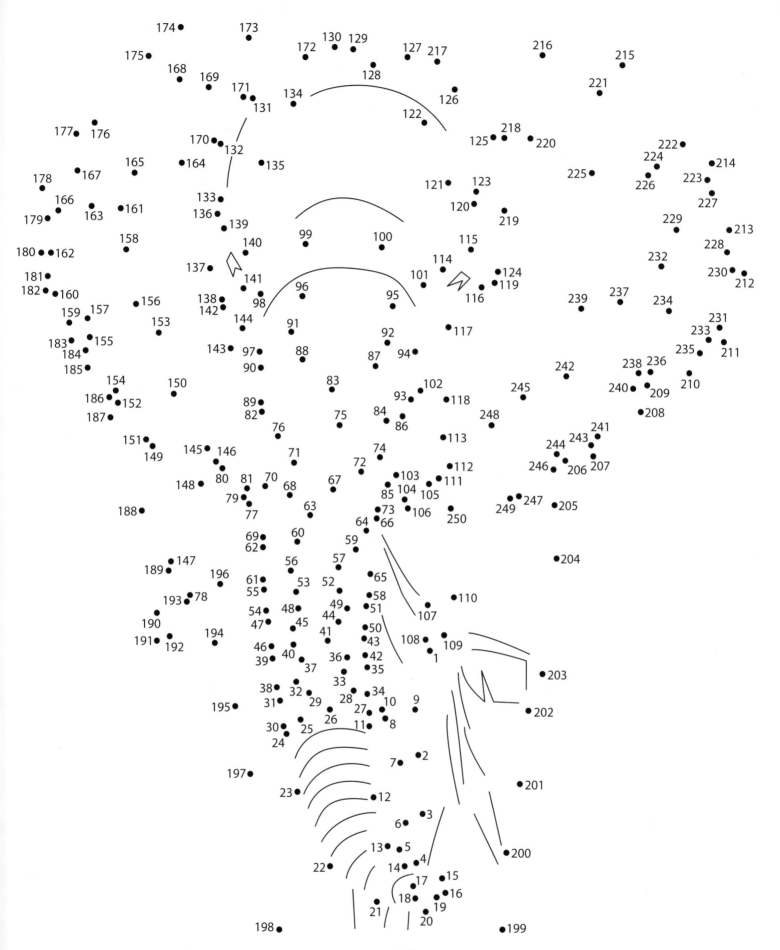

118

WORD SEARCH
SUMMER

```
E S I R N P E L C E N A S P M
P L A Y O C A P V V E T R I E
A A F L O W E R S W R O T P N
K Y L U J R C W E O M K A D F
D E S F E N E A H E W D E V D
N A N O R U T S N H A C H N N
E C L V M H C A O I N I A A A
H F O A E B D E S R E N Y V T
P T I R S E R Y B J D C F A S
W K M S U Y C E U R R I E R D
A B E R H H V N R R A P V A N
S U A D A I E N X O G B E C A
P A B I Y W N C I F F A R T B
S E N F K E Y G A K B E A C H
S H W D E W O O R T S E S O R
```

BANDSTAND	HAY FEVER	SALAD
BARBECUE	JULY	SAND
BEACH	JUNE	SHORTS
CARAVAN	PICNIC	SOMBRERO
DAISY CHAIN	PLAY	TRAFFIC
FISHING	POLLEN	WARMTH
FLOWERS	PROMENADE	WASPS
GARDEN	ROSES	WEATHER

SUDOKU

		5				3		
6	9						1	4
	1		9		3		5	
3				7				1
	6		8		9		2	
9				5				3
	8		3		2		4	
5	2						3	6
		7				8		

2	4	7		6		9		
					4	8		
			2	3		5		
	6							2
3		1				4		7
9							8	
		5		1	2			
		6	9					
		2		8		7	1	9

CROSSWORD

Across

1 Folk singer Phil
5 Fired up
11 In ___ of (for)
12 Grumbler
13 Composer Khachaturian
14 Above the ground
15 Fashion
16 Collected
17 Composer Gustav
19 Alfresco: 2 wds.
21 Infantrymen, initially
24 Dough raiser
25 Happening
27 Part of E.U.: abbr.
28 Finished: 2 wds.
30 Oldsmobile Cutlass ___ (auto of the 1980s and 1990s)
31 Grew very warm: 2 wds.
35 "Jabberwocky" start
38 Disinter
39 "___ Hollers Let Him Go" (Chester B. Himes novel): 2 wds.
40 More authentic
41 Prurient interest
42 Antares and Betelgeuse, e.g.: 2 wds.
43 Little people in "The Time Machine"

Down

1 Norwegian king
2 Opera by Francesco Cavalli
3 "I second that!": 2 wds.
4 Court call
5 Four-time champion of the Australian Open
6 Commerce left to follow its natural course: 2 wds.
7 Dashing Dan was in its logo, initially
8 "…blackbirds baked in ___": 2 wds.
9 Intend
10 Stanley Gardner of mysteries
18 Person who arrives after the expected time
19 Santana hit, "___ Como Va"
20 Little, in Lyons
21 Extremely unpleasant, so to speak: hyph.
22 Debt letters
23 Indy letters
26 Marked by great fruitfulness
29 All-___ (late study sessions, casually)
31 Microbe
32 Clumsy oafs, casually
33 "___ Thing You Do!"
34 Pacific dance
36 Mock phrase of comprehension: 2 wds.
37 Pharaoh, son of Rameses I

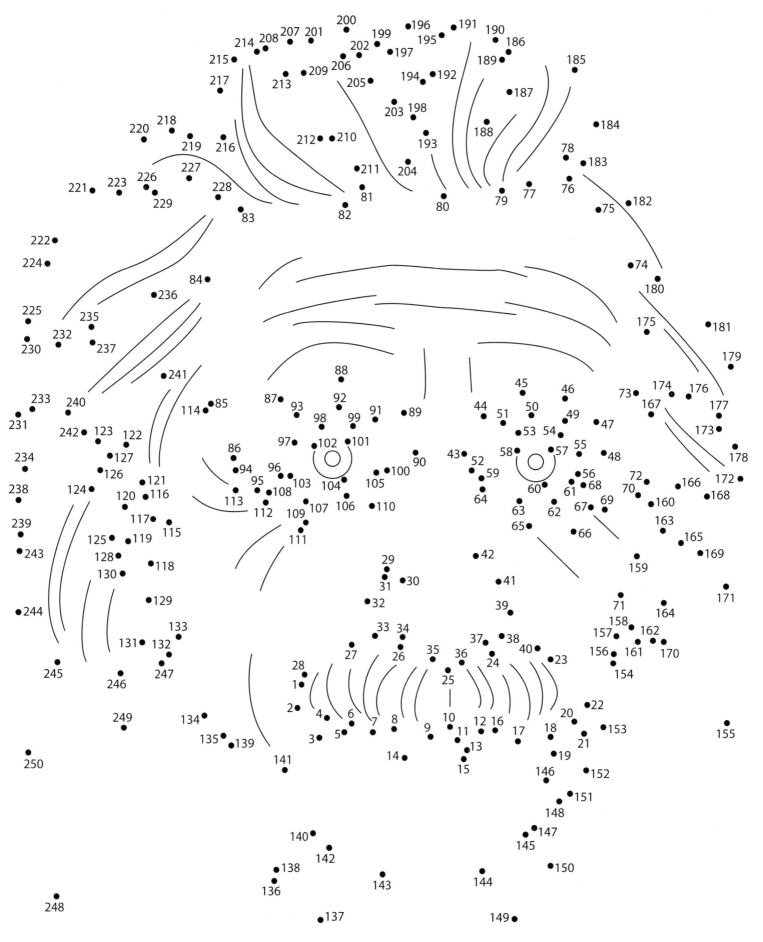

WORD SEARCH
GRASSES

```
H C T I W S S C P B R D G M C
X O F G A K A N G A R O O Z M
O I Y M S Z P Y T A C O S V E
B C R V A N M T E P R Q Z M A
D Q W X R T A B A E U B O A M
Z U E O P N P A C I A R N R A
X A C Q D R H O R R B H Z R N
P K B J N A C R L L M O O A L
K I E Q W K E E C O O W I M T
E N A C S L Y M B B T F H A D
M G E F T T D Z M E E I E G W
A A O A N O O A L S Y H P B X
K O I M E N B L C T W F F T A
T L X Z B K I U B F Q W W V X
S T A O E M E L I C K B Q H L
```

BAMBOO

BARLEY

BEARD

BENT

BROME

CANE

COCKSFOOT

CORN

FESCUE

KANGAROO

KNOT

MAIZE

MARRAM

MEADOW

MELICK

MILLET

MOOR

OATS

PAMPAS

QUAKING

RATTAN

SQUIRRELTAIL

SWITCH

WHEAT

SUDOKU

	3		1		6		7	
4				7				8
		8	5		4	3		
9	1						8	3
		4				9		
2	5						4	1
		6	8		9	2		
7				1				4
	8		2		7		5	

	5		2		3		6	
				6				
2			5		1			8
4	9		7		5		3	2
		2		4		7		
5	7		8		2		9	6
3			1		8			9
				7				
	4		3		9		1	

CROSSWORD

Across

1 "SNL" last name
6 Not yet firm or solid
11 "Actions speak louder than words," for one
12 Carolers' songs
13 Automobile manufactured from 1915 until 1931
14 Cub Scout pack leader
15 Ten Hamiltons: 2 wds.
17 Eighth month of the Jewish calendar
18 Bank acct. report
20 "Novus ___ Seclorum" on a dollar
22 Omega, to an electrician
23 Formally dressed: 3 wds.
26 Letters on a chit
27 WWII craft letters
28 Suffix with serpent
29 Behave in an unrestrained way: 2 wds.
31 Miami Marlins' div.
32 Cake decorator
33 Scrutinize
34 Civil rights org. once led by Stokely Carmichael
36 Galley goof
38 "___ Love" (Pacino film): 2 wds.
40 Scene of WWI fighting
43 Name
44 Ran swiftly
45 Three-time Masters Tournament winner
46 Like craft shows

Down

1 "Take Me Bak ___" (1972 Slade single)
2 Singer Bachman
3 Deprive of church privileges
4 Laughing
5 2002 Literature Nobelist Kertész
6 Actress Merkel
7 Retirement community restriction: 2 wds.
8 Words from one who won't settle: 4 wds.
9 First name in singing
10 Peter the Great, e.g.
16 Keep company
18 Yvette's evening
19 Old word for "you"
21 "Infestation" rock group
23 "Why would ___ to you?": 2 wds.
24 On Hollywood Blvd., e.g.: 2 wds.
25 Rebellious one, maybe
30 Tab alternative: 2 wds.
33 Use a harpoon
34 Fast fleet, briefly
35 No, in Berlin
37 Jewish youth org.
39 Gave a meal to
41 French possessive
42 Dreyer's partner in ice cream

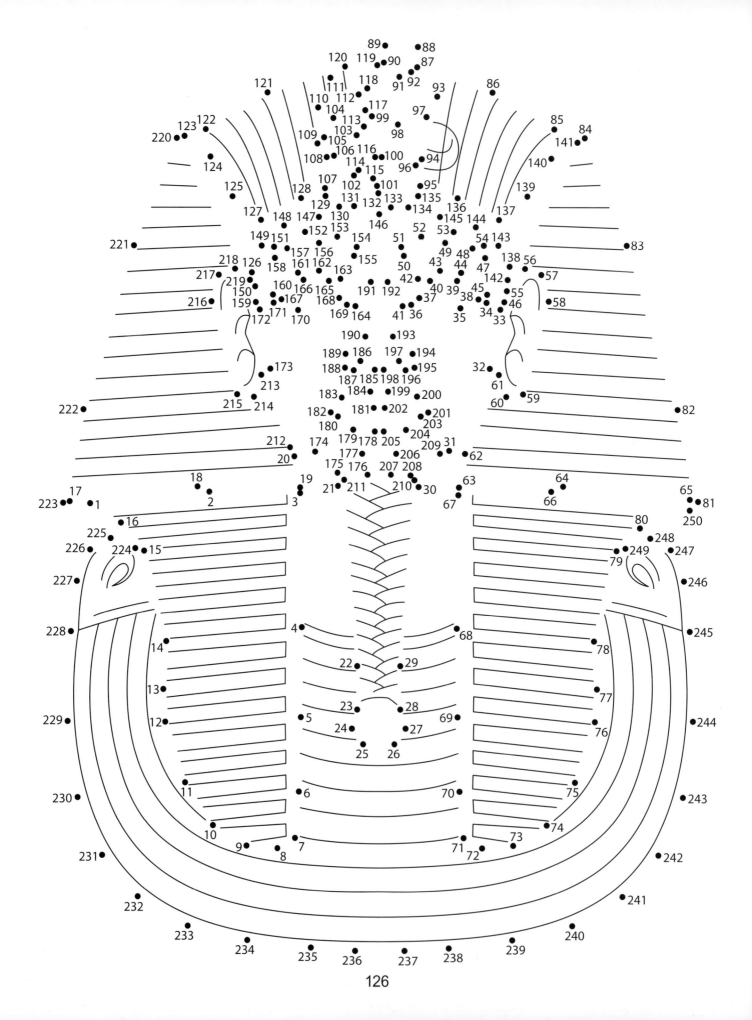

WORD SEARCH
MACHINES

```
D T L L A B N I P Z O S L O T
P I X O W V K T G S E C M G K
L C X A T K E M A N S S N W C
A K V L X L I U G W I I N L I
N E A O E L S L W A W Y N J T
I T J T I A E F L O M L L A
N S Y T G F M Q R I I I D F T
G P A E K N I T T I N G N H S
E R U R W B T Z X A C G Q G O
Y A B Y F A C S I M I L E E R
H D C G R K E Y P U N C H N T
M D L T U R I N G D G W N I C
S I E C I T O F S Z E J N G E
H N U S T F A Q M M X C S M L
K G T H R E S H I N G Q X A E
```

ADDING	KILLING	SAUSAGE
ELECTROSTATIC	KNITTING	SLOT
ENIGMA	LOTTERY	TELETYPE
FACSIMILE	MILITARY	THRESHING
FLYING	MINCING	TICKET
FRUIT	PINBALL	TIME
GAMING	PLANING	TURING
KEYPUNCH	ROWING	WAVE

SUDOKU

4		9		5		8		3
		7	8		2	1		
	1	4				7	3	
8	9						2	1
	6	5				4	8	
		8	7		3	6		
5		6		4		2		7

9	6		5			4		
2				3			7	
		8				5		9
			3			1	9	
	4	7			1			
7		5				9		
	1			6				2
		6			4		1	8

CROSSWORD

Across

1 Santa Claus feature
6 Latin 101 word
10 Cave
11 Pong maker
12 One-time TV workers' union
13 Position with little promise, slangily
14 Squeezing serpent
15 First word of many book titles
17 "Certainement!"
18 Spirits
20 Cape Town country, initially
21 Issue associated with inattentiveness, initially
22 Eats or drinks to excess
24 Freight weight
26 Tone deafness
28 Fewer than twice
31 Actress Carrere
32 Reflexive pronoun
34 One of eight Eng. kings
35 Infant suffix
36 Officiate: abbr.
37 Bottleneck
39 Take as spoils, old-style
41 Prefix with logical
42 Coastal feature
43 Word seg.
44 French cup

Down

1 "___ Black Sheep" (kids' rhyme): 2 wds.
2 Clasp lovingly in one's arms
3 Hang up a picture, e.g.: 4 wds.
4 Grammar-school trio, initially
5 Decease
6 Airport service letters
7 Some army officers: 2 wds.
8 Pique
9 Shinbones
11 Flier Earhart
16 Metal item used to reinforce the sole of a boot
19 Take too much of, briefly: 2 wds.
23 Non-profit, voluntary citizens' groups, initially
25 Ex ___ (from nothing)
26 They produce mushroom clouds, briefly: 2 wds.
27 "In the Heat of the Night" star Poitier
29 Whence Henry VIII's Anne hailed
30 Decadent
33 Worth
38 Sermon subj.
40 Alfonso XIII's queen

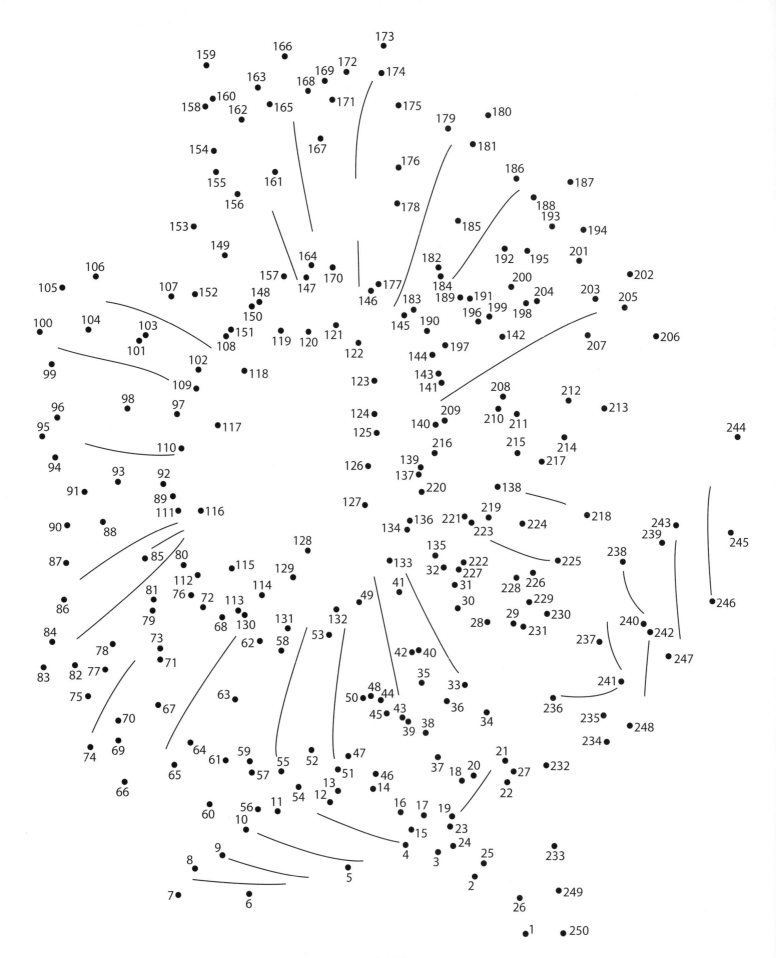

WORD SEARCH
NUTS AND SEEDS

```
W A L T N U G Y R E L E C V Y
R F C A R A W A Y L X T F D S
M E U Y E P B P I L E T E B L
Z B D S A E O D E C A S H E W
H T U N E N I P F C R M F M B
X Z B A A R I E P L A Q L A O
P U M P K I N S I Y R N A S C
T D G J A N R Z E E G L X E A
C O N K E R A O S O M T R S R
Z D M L V R N O C O C U W T D
N C I U B A N N N T N N N U A
T U N A E P A D V F O O I N M
C O B N U T T L O T P C M L O
Z U I E A K T E B R Z O U A M
C M U N I N O W H C E C C W O
```

ALMOND	CELERY	FLAX
ANISE	COBNUT	PEANUT
ANNATTO	COCONUT	PECAN
BETEL	CONKER	PINE NUT
BRAZIL	CORIANDER	POPPY
CARAWAY	CUMIN	PUMPKIN
CARDAMOM	DILL	SESAME
CASHEW	FENNEL	WALNUT

SUDOKU

2					8	3		5
	9	7						2
		8			2		1	
					4	5		
	6						4	
		3	8					
	8		3			6		
1						2	9	
5		6	1					7

5								8
	4		3		9		7	
6	2						3	4
		7	9	5	2	3		
		5	8	6	1	4		
2	3						8	1
	1		7		4		6	
7								3

CROSSWORD

Across

1 Quick on the uptake
6 "Six ___, half a dozen…": 2 wds.
11 "Walk Away ___" (1966 hit)
12 Mutineer
13 Hint
14 Dental filling
15 Supplementary
17 Hostess and diplomat Mesta
18 Olympic boxer Riddick
21 One-named Tejano singer
25 Old spy org.
26 Walk softly
27 Apostle whose feast day is December 27th: 2 wds.
31 "High Noon" marshal
32 Cousin of a raccoon
34 Adversary, opponent
39 Film award
40 First name in beauty
41 They award degs.
42 Religious paintings: var.
43 Plain for all ___: 2 wds.
44 Certain fraction

Down

1 Miss in Mexico: abbr.
2 Group
3 Take out ___ in the paper (publicize): 2 wds.
4 Formula for cooking a dish
5 Calvin of the PGA
6 Maryland's state bird
7 Herb that tastes like licorice
8 "___-Di, ___-Da" (Beatles song): 2 wds.
9 Patricia of "The Subject Was Roses"
10 England's Isle of ___
16 Collection agcy.
18 Diddley and Derek
19 East, to Germans
20 NYT rival
22 Clean air org.
23 Bert Bobbsey's twin sister
24 Cooler in the summer
28 Series of eight musical notes
29 Raspy
30 Be a henpecker
31 Nastassja of "Tess"
33 Auto wheel adjustment: hyph.
34 "It comes ___ surprise to me…": 2 wds.
35 Mark Harmon series on CBS
36 Have ___ good authority: 2 wds.
37 On its way
38 "Entertainment Tonight" co-host John
39 Fully anesthetized

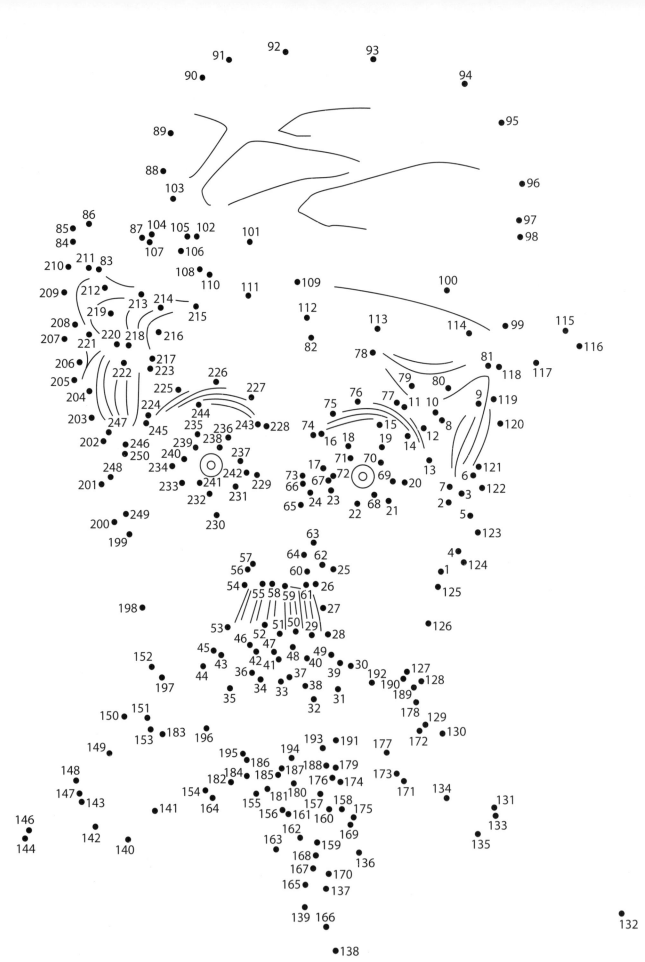

134

WORD SEARCH
"M" TO "M"

```
M E D I U M N V H J D J M M Z
U E M N X M U X O V Z F I U I
T M D S B W U A V R V G L D G
N M L O I V M E H F N T S N M
E A H I M P U U L C M C U A A
M E M E F Y O C S O S J M R L
O L A I F O Q R D E S R S O C
M S R W L D R R P M U U E M O
M T X V S L Y C B A Y M A E L
E R I M A T E R I A L I S M M
T O S H R Y Z N S M V A A M M
O M M A Y H E M N N I G M A C
N N M I N I M U M I N X D H P
Y M O O N B E A M U U A A F M
M U C I D O M E M E M M H M G
```

MADAM   MAUSOLEUM   MILLENNIUM

MAELSTROM   MAXIM   MINIMUM

MAGNUM   MAYHEM   MODEM

MALAPROPISM   MEDIUM   MODICUM

MALCOLM   MEERSCHAUM   MOMENTUM

MARTYRDOM   MEMORANDUM   MOONBEAM

MARXISM   METONYM   MUSEUM

MATERIALISM   MICROFILM   MUSLIM

SUDOKU

		5	2		7	3		
7			4		6			8
	4						7	
6	1		9		4		3	5
9	3		1		8		4	6
	8					2		
2			5		3			1
		1	7		9	6		

6	4			5			1	9
3			1		9			4
	1						8	
			4		8			
	9						2	
			9		5			
	2						6	
5			6		2			3
8	3			4			9	7

CROSSWORD

Across

1 Good name for a Dalmatian
5 Exhausted person's utterance: 2 wds.
11 Common cat food flavor
12 Port city and resort of southern Spain
13 Dentist's request
14 Causes to be suspended
15 Old, in Aberdeen
16 James in many westerns
17 Rodrigo Díaz de Vivar: 2 wds.
19 Peak
22 Buffet
26 Make illegal payment in exchange for favors
27 Secret store
28 Others, to Ovid
29 "___ Bells" (Christmas song)
30 Truckers, usually, for short
32 Attack, as a predator does: 2 wds.
35 ___ one's time (wait for the right moment)
39 Lubricant container
40 Certain plaintiff, at law
41 Slender and elegant
42 Dunaway who played Bonnie
43 Most docile
44 Moat: var.

Down

1 Ancient colonnade
2 Chinese appetizers: 2 wds.
3 First-year J.D. student: 2 wds.
4 Vehicle for two: 2 wds.
5 Collision
6 Polynesian language
7 Children's party game: 2 wds.
8 Moderate
9 Forever and a day
10 ITAR-___ news agency
18 Tall tale
19 Maria Contreras-Sweet's organization, initially
20 Browser bookmark, initially
21 Nintendo free-form personal avatar
23 Arrhythmia detector, initially
24 U.S./Canadian sporting grp. since 1936
25 Bruce or Spike
27 Fig. with a diameter
29 Female donkey
31 Sailing vessels
32 Washington or Denver newspaper
33 1972 Kentucky Derby winner ___ Ridge
34 Kind of school: abbr.
36 Golfer Aoki
37 Former pashas of Algiers
38 Some shoe sizes

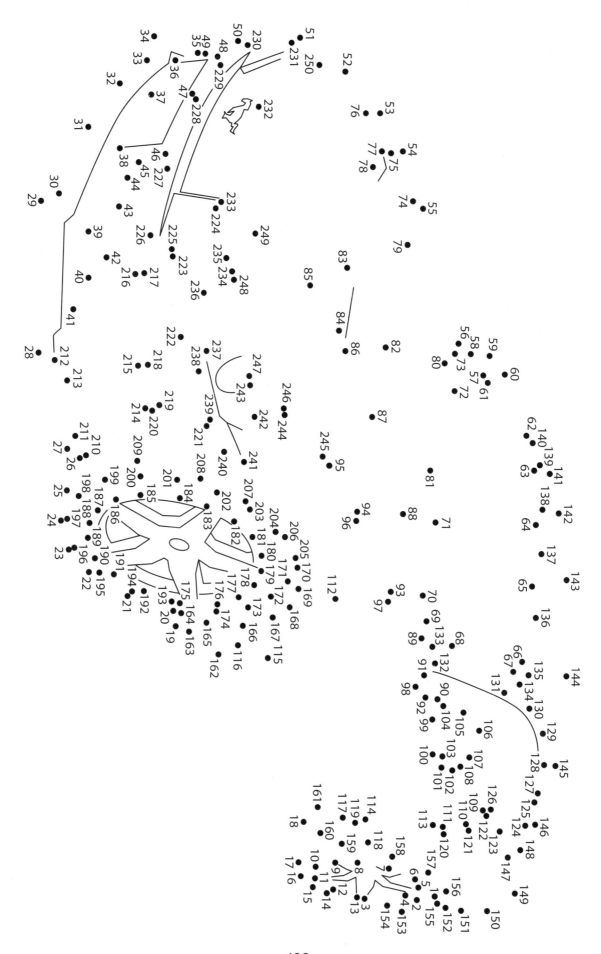

WORD SEARCH
PAIRS OF THINGS

```
U G Y V E X S Q N B Z H L J B
W D A Y Q P X G R J O B S L P
T C E E Q P W A N L P A D U Y
M E C S L A C K S I N A K N S
C I E I M E S P Y D G T K G B
D U E F S S J E A N S G N S F
S R S J L R G L T I Y O E L W
S E O R S E S V A T F I L S
S P T H U P H S S X K P C D E
C R O T I P D T U H F S N P S
N E E Q O I S N F L O A Z W S
S G S C K L C A O Y H R K P A
B A E S N S U P P N D Z T K L
A P Y U Q I S C Y B S K M S G
S R E K A E P S D U O L P I C
```

BRACES   JEANS   SHOES

CULOTTES   LEGGINGS   SHORTS

DICE   LOUDSPEAKERS   SKATES

EYES   LUNGS   SLACKS

FEET   PANTS   SLIPPERS

FLIP-FLOPS   PINCERS   SPURS

GLASSES   PLIERS   STAYS

HANDS   SANDALS   TONGS

SUDOKU

	8							6
					1	9		
7	2			5				
		6			9			8
3	5			7			2	9
2			3			4		
				2			8	1
		3	4					
5							7	

4								7
		6	5		7	9		
	1		4		8		2	
3	7		2		5		4	9
9	8		1		3		5	6
	6		3		4		9	
		2	7		1	5		
1								8

CROSSWORD

Across

1 Thompson in "Pollock"
5 Actress Richards or singer Grande
11 Horn sound
12 Internet novice, slangily
13 Oxygen, simply: 2 wds.
14 Publications in electronic form: hyph.
15 Author's pseudonym: 2 wds.
17 Something to lend or bend
18 Chip ingredient
23 Etched: abbr.
25 Symphonic conclusion
26 Branches bound together as fuel
28 Arabian Peninsula nation
29 Roman emperor defeated by Vitellius
30 What's expected
31 Turn to stone
33 Paddle lookalike
36 Move with exaggerated motions
38 Residence of the president of France
42 Turn on a pivot
43 Person who loves books
44 Horse feed
45 Adds more lubricant
46 ___ 'Pea (Popeye's charge)

Down

1 Steplike part of a mine
2 Maori canoe
3 Utterly
4 Immensely: 2 wds.
5 Weak
6 Riot
7 WWII battle site, for short
8 Classification system for blood
9 Suffix with nud or kibbutz
10 Loser to D.D.E.
16 Busy exec.'s need
19 Patisserie employee
20 Like some marriages: hyph.
21 Poem of praise
22 Teardrop-shaped Indian bread
24 Queen who wrote "Leap of Faith"
26 Smart dresser
27 Lingered over lunch, e.g.
28 Fluctuate: hyph.
30 Super Bowl players, briefly
32 "___ Pretty" (song from "West Side Story"): 2 wds.
34 Intense
35 Peewee or Della
37 Service club units, initially
38 To do it is human
39 Jeans brand
40 Retired basketballer Ming
41 "Star Wars" project of the 1980s

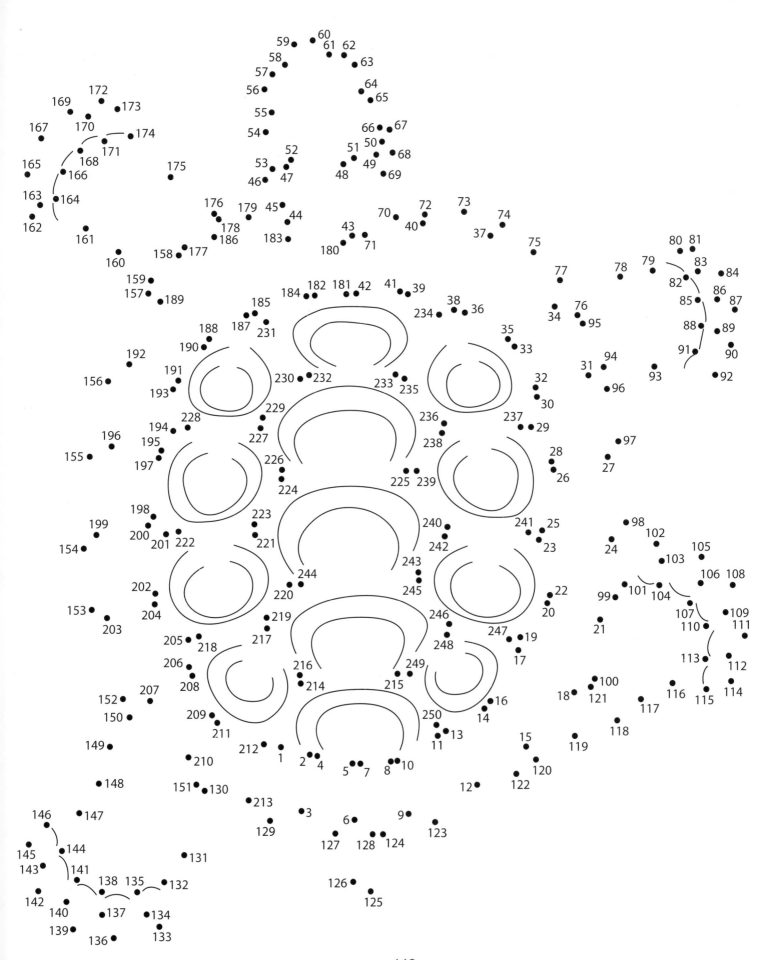

142

WORD SEARCH
NORTHERN IRELAND

```
D C X M K T D M O U R N E Y D
R L G H H U R O M F T I D M M
O A X N N O D M I V M A S I A
M U D L W O C X O K E A N R B
A D O K R U J R M K I Q A T B
R Y M D R O G N A B G L R N E
A E N B H C N N G I G U R A L
C U B S X G Y L H J G V U E F
D E Z M P Z A P E M B A C Q A
Y A N A O H A M N J P V V C S
L R X O S C G A R V A G H O T
N B W I R I E U A A H H P R N
U W L E O Y N P L L I H C I R
O G O A N O T N I F D H I Y P
E K U D W G S S E R D R A M U
```

ANTRIM	CURRAN	KEADY
ARDRESS	DOWN	KILREA
ARMAGH	DROMARA	LARNE
BANGOR	DUNDROD	MOURNE
BELFAST	DUNLOY	NEWRY
CLAUDY	EGLISH	OMAGH
COMBER	FINTONA	RICHILL
CRAIGAVON	GARVAGH	TYRONE

SUDOKU

	4			8	2	9		
	2	1		9				
			6					8
					8			5
	9			4			2	
7			3					
3					5			
				2		4	1	
		6	1	3			7	

9			4		8			3
	4	8				7	2	
3								6
	6			1			5	
2			6		7			1
	3			2			7	
7								5
	1	6				8	9	
5			8		9			4

CROSSWORD

Across

1 Greed is one
4 Driver's ID: abbr.
7 Jump
10 Pub pint
11 ___ moment: 2 wds.
12 Pac.'s counterpart
13 Bridge of arches
15 Opposite of alt: Ger.
16 Architect Saarinen who designed Washington Dulles' main terminal
17 Frozen cause of water blockage: 2 wds.
19 Prepare for dinner, say: 2 wds.
21 Contract endorser
24 "Murphy's Romance" director Martin
27 Staff leaders
28 Ball game from Italy: var.
29 New Rochelle, New York college
30 Dinner table linen
31 Fighting ___ (Big Ten team)
33 Tiredness after a long flight: 2 wds.
35 Peter Fonda's golden part
39 Swiss canton
40 Geometric figure
42 Actress Ullmann
43 George Burns role
44 Ring cheer
45 "___-haw!"
46 Metallica's first U.S. hit
47 KLM competitor

Down

1 File menu command
2 "Out on the lawn ___ in bed": Auden: 2 wds.
3 Impending
4 Lucy who played one of "Charlie's Angels"
5 Carve
6 Unexpected condition
7 Select carefully for a particular purpose
8 "Cup ___" (1970s Don Williams song): 2 wds.
9 Pudding fruit
14 Waterloo
18 Soft silvery metallic element
20 1950s presidential race inits.
21 ___-fi
22 Labor group initials
23 Case of nouns and pronouns indicating possession
25 1999 AT&T purchase
26 Canister
28 Bristol-Myers roll-on brand
30 Almost: 2 wds.
32 "Key ___"
33 Summer month
34 Great Lakes city
36 Corp. takeovers
37 Opera singer Beal
38 Mexican men, colloquially
41 Poem often about a person

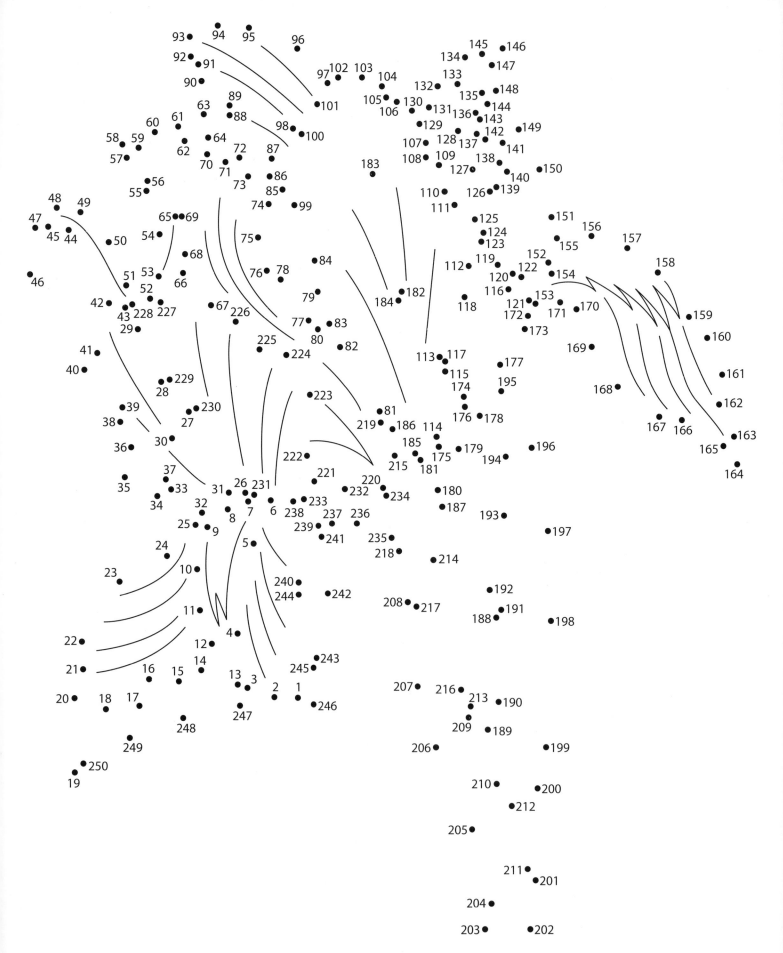

WORD SEARCH
"A" WORDS

```
E I B A Y T S T D A T A D I A
L T Y M R A S A S S E M B L E
A A U M S Y V U S N I K A A J
Z U I T A R I O G N I V B V T
U G I D S W C H U U O A R A M
R M D P I A A T C C A F G L N
E E L A A N T S E R H T A A Y
D N A U I F G T D A U E R N G
I T Z A A S S V M C H R P C N
S A T K I T A S A U H W Y H I
A T E J A R E G R P I A A E H
A I C K K P A L E A G R B A C
M O I X A P P P I A A D T S A
H N A G E A A L C E F S H A U
A D M X A Z E X Y B R B P A A
```

AARDVARK	ARMY	AUGUST
ACHING	ASIDE	AVALANCHE
ADDED	ASSEMBLE	AVOCET
AFTERWARDS	ASTUTE	AVOUCH
AGAINST	ATELIER	AWRY
AGAPE	ATRIUM	AXIOM
AIDING	ATTAIN	AZTEC
APPLY	AUGMENTATION	AZURE

SUDOKU

		6			9			
				4	1		8	3
								1
		5	6			1	7	
3				1				4
	8	1			7	2		
2								
8	1		9	3				
			5			7		

	6						1	
		3	4		6	8		
9			2		7			5
1	5		6		2		9	8
4	2		3		8		5	7
6			7		1			3
		9	8		4	5		
	7						4	

CROSSWORD

Across

1 Attempt computer crimes
5 Look up to
11 Et ___
12 Butcher's tool: 2 wds.
13 Former Chevy
14 Fight
15 "___ et labora" (pray and work)
16 Commuter rail company, initially
17 Jazz pianist Chick
19 Members of a pride
23 Env. stuffer
24 Vertical part of a plane: hyph.
25 Perceive
27 Sandberg of baseball
28 MC's spiel
30 Weapons systems provider, initially
31 Feudal lord
32 Grave robber
35 Girl's name
37 FDR home loan org.
38 "Jason Lives" in "Friday the Thirteenth," e.g.: 2 wds.
41 Shirt button
42 Possessive pronoun
43 Delicate
44 Surgeon's tool
45 Millstone

Down

1 Devastation
2 Oldsmobile model
3 Tube of finely ground tobacco wrapped in paper
4 "Trust in Me" singing snake
5 Prefix with lateral
6 At great cost
7 Female head of a family or tribe
8 "The Addams Family" cousin
9 North Carolina capital: abbr.
10 River of Devon
16 Lancelot du ___ (knight of the Round Table)
18 Full of vim and vigor
20 Pain-blocking drug
21 Palindromic diarist
22 Chicago to Tampa dir.
25 Null
26 Ogre of Japanese folklore
29 Works, collectively
30 ___ Khan
33 ___ Torch, national symbol of Tanzania
34 ___-slipper
36 Grocery shopper's reference
38 Club headed by the Bakkers, initially
39 "So it's you!"
40 "You eediot!" speaker
41 ___ Tomé and Principe (African republic)

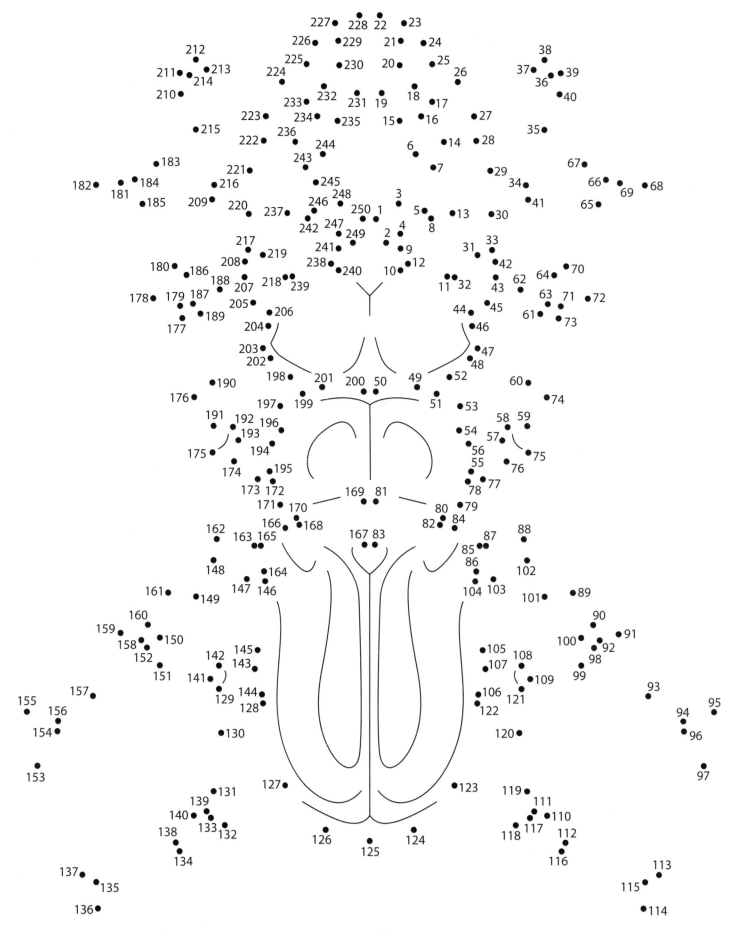

150

WORD SEARCH
CAKES

```
T E N D C N J E L B R A M S I
O U A Q I H T N A R R U C A D
F T N S W P E T H I E Q K N C
E R I L T W T E O S S D P N E
I A Q C A E P Q S E K O N E T
R K S F N W R T I E U O F N U
Y N J B A T D N A N O F R E N
L E U L M A W N D R O L E L O
E R C F Z O H G A C O E G L C
G D H C R C M C N E F G N O O
N U E B A T A F O I T N I T C
A B R S T M K R P M D A G S S
R O R T Z A B U Q V Q D D N A
O Y Y M U F F I N L A Y E R Z
A R I E D A M T O R R A C W M
```

ANGEL FOOD	CURRANT	MARBLE
BATTENBURG	DATE AND	MOCHA
BROWNIES	WALNUT	MUFFIN
CARROT	EASTER	ORANGE
CHEESE	FRUIT	POUND
CHERRY	GINGER	RAISIN
COCONUT	LAYER	STOLLEN
COFFEE	MACAROON	WEDDING
	MADEIRA	

SUDOKU

5	6						9	4
		3				2		
		8	5		6	3		
3				4				9
		4	2		9	7		
2				7				1
		1	6		8	5		
		9				1		
7	2						6	8

2								4
8			5		9			2
	9	5				1	6	
		2		1		6		
1			4		6			3
		4		3		7		
	4	3				8	9	
7			9		8			5
6								7

CROSSWORD

Across

1 City in Israel: 2 wds.

8 Partner of poivre

11 "West Side Story" song

12 Do-say link: 2 wds.

13 "The ___ you!": 2 wds.

14 Atlas abbr.

15 Singer Tennille

16 ___ Fail, Irish coronation stone

17 More than hate

20 Mountain Community of the Tejon Pass, Calif.

22 Environmental prefix

23 Miss ___ (TV psychic)

24 Echo: 2 wds.

29 List enders, briefly

30 Pretoria's country letters

31 Sore spot

33 Hebrew letter

35 "Obviously!"

36 Old English letters

38 Trick taker, often

39 Great Plains tribe

43 ___ for Lion: 2 wds.

44 Spring signs

45 Release, with "out"

46 School

Down

1 Cap worn by a dervish

2 Funnyman Philips

3 Albanian coin

4 Ratio words: 2 wds.

5 Golfer's accessory

6 Sacred symbol

7 Popular ice cream flavor

8 Windsurfer's equipment

9 "The Devil's Disciple" girl

10 Eye shadow shade

17 Atmospheric prefix

18 Letters used (by some) for dates

19 Bridal container: 2 wds.

21 Brain test initials

23 Hundredths of a dollar, briefly

25 Summer, in St-Malo

26 Area of land

27 Language name suffix

28 Glasgow denial

31 Former Secretary of the Interior Stewart

32 Daughter of Ball and Arnaz

33 SeaWorld attraction

34 Chaudfroid glaze

37 A famous Scott

40 Yoga teacher Brett

41 Sellout

42 Suffix with lact-

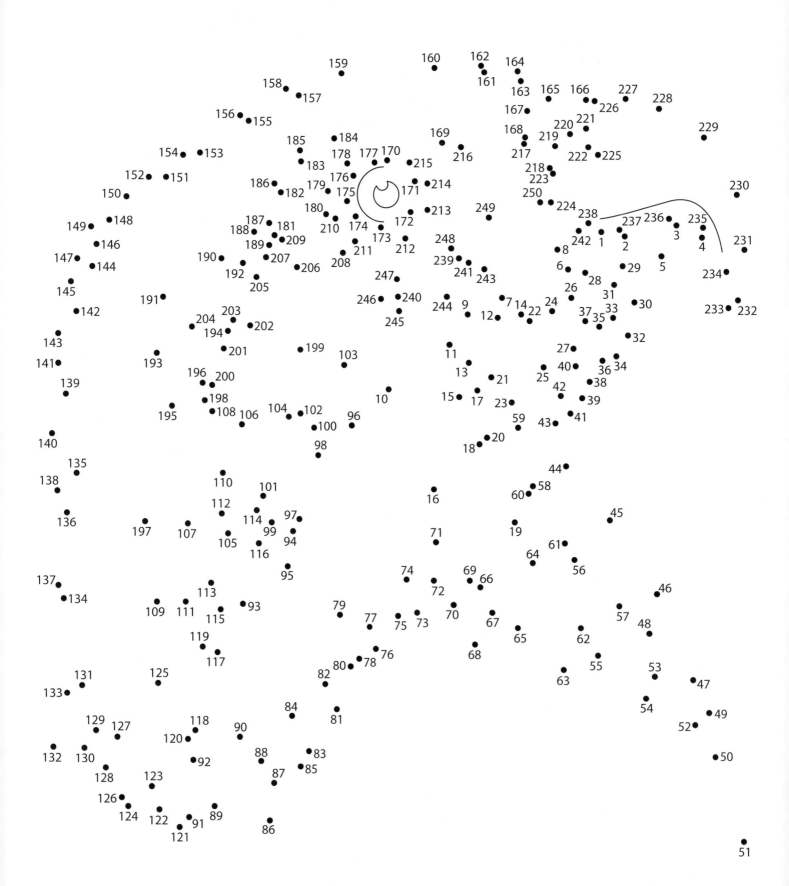

WORD SEARCH
COINS

```
P E V M D Y L Z Q N E W H N S
E S O O O V R O A L L F A S D
B G N I L L I H S O B P H U R
S K Q D L A Q D P Y O B C I Q
P Z B O A E Z E H L N A H R C
T O P R R R N H E Z T M N A E
S H U E L N D O T A O R G N B
T T A N Y S N B Z R X E I E K
N O A L D S G O H G O C E D X
A W C T E Y U L A B K X R T F
Z A O S E R I G X E D F E K L
E E N R A R N E L H T Z V U O
B M X G C B E U R E P P O C R
O I E K E F A N O M H J S P I
L D H J O L Z K Q S E S T X N
```

ANGEL	FLORIN	PENNY
BEZANT	GROAT	POUND
COPPER	GUINEA	REAL
CROWN	MOIDORE	SHILLING
DENARIUS	NAPOLEON	SOU
DIME	NICKEL	SOVEREIGN
DOLLAR	NOBLE	STATER
DUCAT	OBOL	THALER

SUDOKU

9		4				1		5
8		3	5	9			7	
				4				
					6		3	1
	1						8	
6	8		1					
				1				
	3			2	4	6		9
4		1				8		2

				5				
		8	2		6	5		
	2		8		9		4	
	7	1	3		8	6	2	
2				7				3
	8	3	4		2	1	5	
	6		9		4		1	
		7	6		1	9		
				3				

CROSSWORD

Across

1 Waters

6 Scoop

10 Kate Middleton's sister

11 "You ___ lot to me!": 2 wds.

13 Expected hopefully

15 Fictional govt. agency in "24," initially

16 Retrovirus component, initially

17 Milieu for the Boston Bruins

18 Control and make use of natural resources

20 Fannie or Ginnie follower

21 Cube creator Rubik

22 Robin Williams' role in a 1982 movie: inits., 2 wds.

24 It may be bid

26 Dye obtain from lichens

29 Future atty.'s exam

33 Open tract

34 Holding conservative views: hyph.

36 Harvard deg.

37 Middle grade

38 Child care expert LeShan

39 He prepares places of burial

42 Withers

43 Mark ___, J.R. in "Barnaby Jones"

44 Sported, as golf's green jacket

45 Core

Down

1 Attack helicopter

2 Albanian currency

3 Good news on Wall Street

4 Set of functions in computing, initially

5 Start of a French oath

6 Stalemate

7 PBS benefactor

8 Youngest daughter of the prophet Muhammad

9 Kind of garage: hyph.

12 Take ___ breath: 2 wds.

14 Gradually implanted

19 Genesis skipper

23 Deceive

25 Bishopric

26 Cosmonaut Atkov and designer Cassini

27 Sketched afresh

28 Classic Chevrolet

30 Encircled and attacked

31 Swedish astronomer Celsius

32 Attack: 2 wds.

35 Religious doctrine

40 Neighbor of N.H.

41 Alphabetical sequence

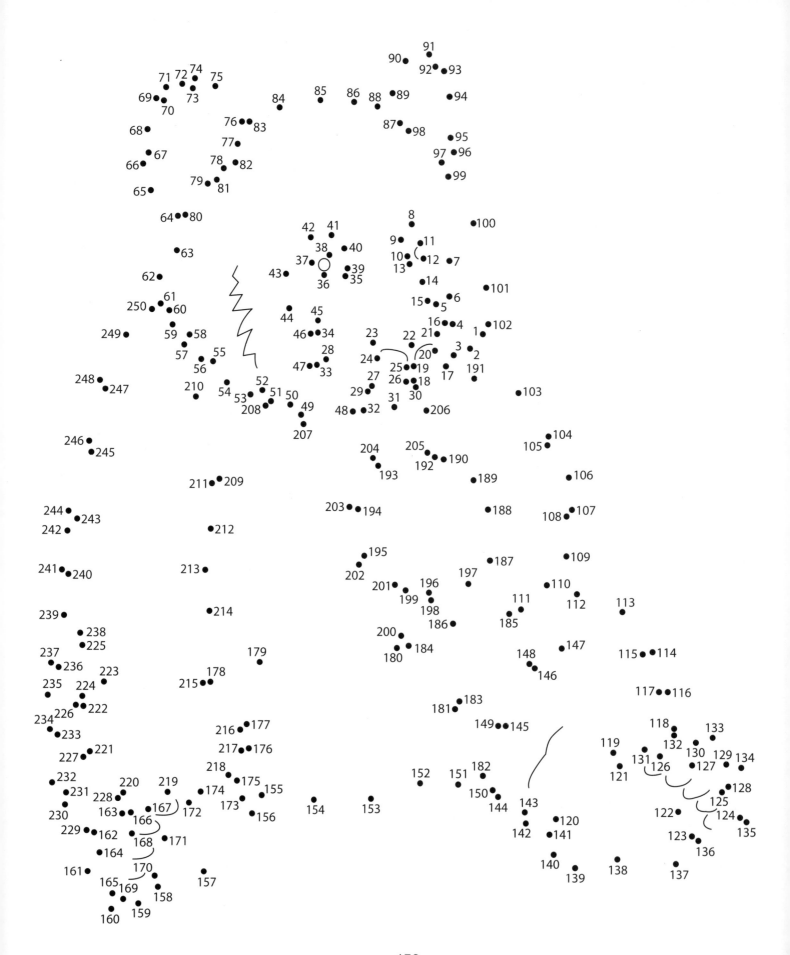

WORD SEARCH
SO BAD

```
J L S R O F G S Y R X V R D L
D P I E O Y N U T W G S D O U
Y I C V B B L O S R Z U D C F
A D S Z E U V I A M I O I O N
W C U A F F Y C N C C V C N I
F Y E T G W G I M O L E N T S
U J R J R R R N R U G I A E O
L U N O O W E R F U H H R M Y
H C N C S D U E U A A C Y P T
S G C B S P N P A O S S V T H
I O U Z T A R L Z B T I I I G
L T R A B U S I V E L M L B U
L O S I M M O R A L Y E E L A
E D E K C I W B B R O T T E N
H V D Y L L A C S A R B E L G
```

ABUSIVE	GHASTLY	PERNICIOUS
AWFUL	GROSS	RANCID
BANEFUL	HELLISH	RASCALLY
CONTEMPTIBLE	HURTFUL	ROTTEN
CORRUPT	IMMORAL	SINFUL
CURSED	MISCHIEVOUS	VILE
DISAGREEABLE	NASTY	WICKED
EVIL	NAUGHTY	WRONG

SUDOKU

		9				6		
7	5			2			1	3
		8	5		6	4		
8				6				9
			2		4			
9				1				7
		2	1		3	7		
5	6			4			3	8
		1				9		

	3		6		7		5	
	7	5		2		4	6	
1								7
		7		1		8		
			9		4			
		2		8		7		
9								4
	2	1		3		6	8	
	4		7		8		3	

CROSSWORD

Across

1 Avian chatterbox
6 "Wheel of Fortune" host
11 Basketball Hall of Famer Thomas
12 South American animal
13 Blessing
15 "I'm not really impressed"
16 Little seal
17 Light units: abbr.
18 Overshoot a puck
19 Liq. measures
20 Disney deer
21 Highway
23 Crumbs
24 Words to live by
26 Part of an Asian capital's name
29 Acted as an umpire, so to speak
33 Rescuer of Odysseus, in myth
34 Army E-3, initially
35 Shiba ___ (dog breed)
36 Kicks
37 Teacher of Samuel
38 ___'wester
39 Elmore Leonard novel about a former 1960s radical: 2 wds.
42 "___ Hold You" (Bow Wow song of 2005): 2 wds.
43 Songwriter Greenwich
44 Some hooks
45 ___ 180 (reverses course): 2 wds.

Down

1 Algonquian tribe
2 Look
3 Code
4 Berne's river
5 Burger King sandwich
6 High-fives
7 Key abbr.
8 Prison warden
9 Measure
10 "Dust in the Wind" group
14 Caterpillar of the future
22 Command level: abbr.
23 Gut reaction?
25 Definite, unquestionable
26 Horsefeathers
27 Habituates
28 Compositions for nine musicians
30 Dramatic or exciting conclusion
31 Gourmet mushrooms
32 "The Bamboo Saucer" star Dan
34 Lap dogs
40 Parisian soul
41 "Xanadu" rock group, initially

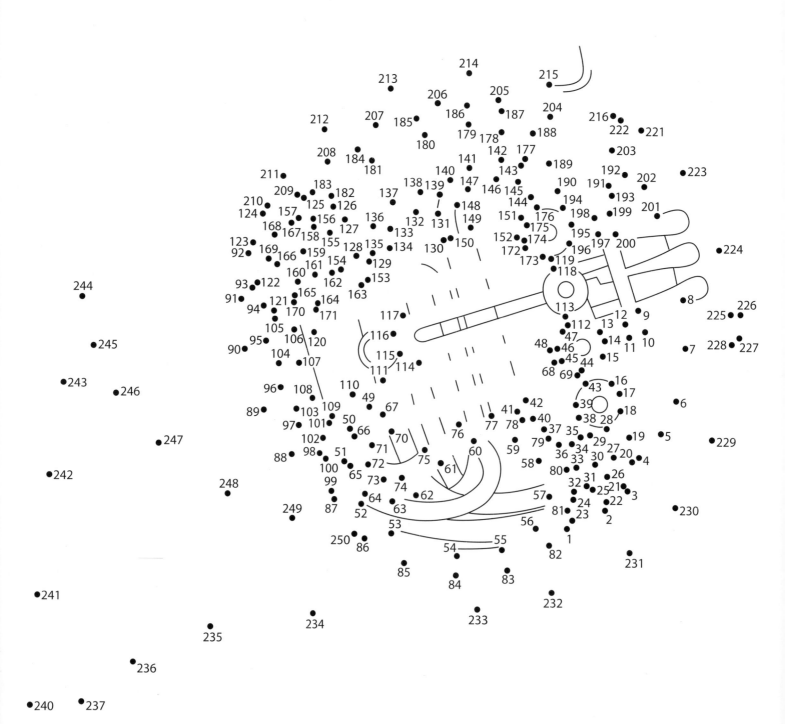

WORD SEARCH
TITLES

```
Y S E Y A I Z M B V Y N Z H G
G M E O U Q S M K O D U K E T
N A C O L O N E L R A B B I F
I D N F A G V A M A D E D U Q
K A I A O Q R I U C M S N S P
W M R T U E S E A V I W E S O
V A P H N T N P A L R B R E H
N R T E E T I A R A Z E H S
I Q G R P A D R E X L X V C I
Q U X L I I O I Y L X Q E U B
J E E N O P R B S T U N R D H
A S J U R K T J Q E O A G O C
B S R O R E P M E R R F R V R
T I C M O G O N A W R P M F A
M M P H L N S B L C F Q E B U
```

ADMIRAL	EARL	MISS
ARCHBISHOP	EMPEROR	MISTER
BARON	FATHER	PADRE
CAPTAIN	FRAULEIN	PRESIDENT
COLONEL	GENERAL	PRINCE
CORPORAL	KING	QUEEN
DUCHESS	MADAM	RABBI
DUKE	MARQUESS	REVEREND

SUDOKU

				5	8			
	2	6		4	7	1	8	
4								
6				8		9		
		2	4		3	6		
		9		2				3
								9
	3	7	9	1		2	5	
			5	3				

			3		6		9	
5		3		2				
1			9					
			4				8	7
2				3				5
3	7			9				
					1			3
				5		6		1
	4		8		3			

CROSSWORD

Across

1 Heart

6 Leading Romantic poet

11 Pick any number from ___ ten: 2 wds.

12 1991 Nicholson Baker book about his fascination with John Updike: 3 wds.

13 Clueless: 2 wds.

14 Swing wildly

15 Goes ballistic: 3 wds.

17 Whole mess of, slangily

18 Central European

20 ___-Lorraine

25 Great Barrier Island of New Zealand

27 Expenditure

28 "Turandot" and "Tosca"

30 Nose: comb. form

31 Exemplary, as a citizen

33 "Of course"

38 Error's partner

39 Certain missile

40 Rosario ___, former Treasurer of the U.S.A.

41 Zombie novelist Brian

42 "If ___ A Boy" (Beyoncé song): 2 wds.

43 Enough, in French

Down

1 Ruth's birthplace

2 Like some airports: abbr.

3 Barren

4 Sweat, so to speak: 2 wds.

5 Best man's recitation

6 City near Niagara Falls

7 River that forms most of the China-North Korea border

8 Cell messenger letters

9 Dog of the funnies

10 Nothing on a soccer field

16 Simile phrase: 2 wds.

18 ___ Paulo

19 Cut (off)

21 Guarantees

22 Olympians

23 Special effects used in "Avatar," e.g.

24 Almost forever

26 "When We Were Very Young" poet: inits., 2 wds.

29 Father's boy

32 He's coached Bears and Saints

33 Doodle

34 Shamrock spot

35 O.K.

36 Pool division

37 California's Santa ___ Valley

38 "That's more than I needed to hear!," initially

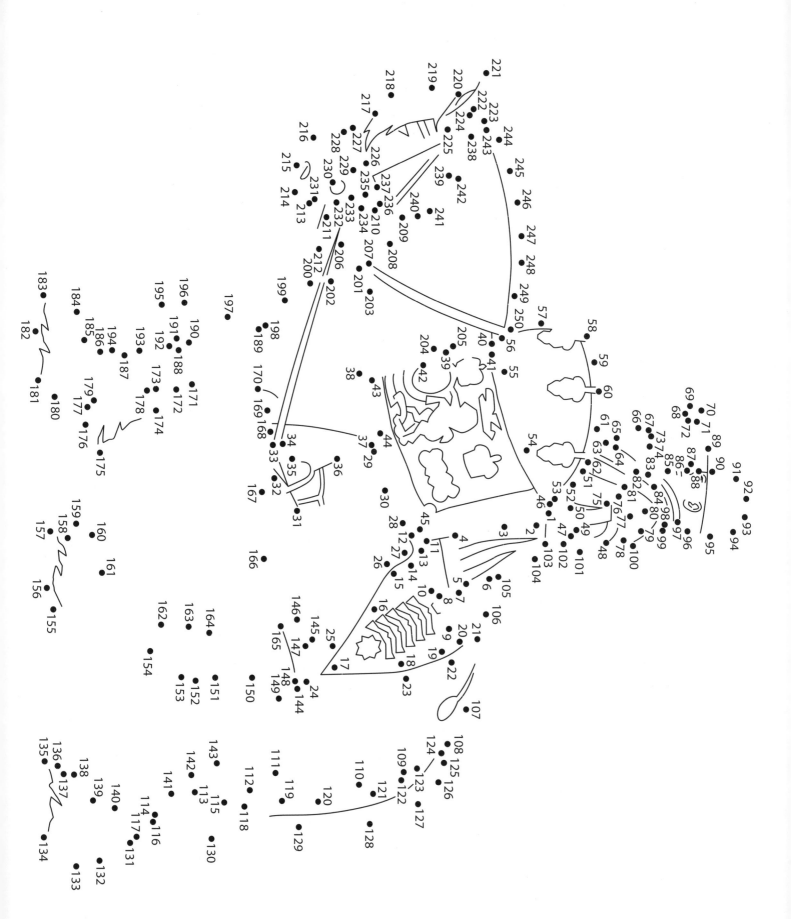

166

WORD SEARCH
CONTAINERS

```
B U A X O B H W O D A O W A E
G U J K N C T E K S A B N I I
C O E C U R A N H R E K C O L
H G X O A K B M U R D S A W C
A D P Y P H S T E I N G E T A
V T A R S I N E F T E L B O G
E L E I Y N C R E P M A H P R
R T D S R H R V P E R S P R I
S P N P A B F E T J A S L E E
A H U A T C W S D U D P P W V
C C U E H E F S C F L G Q O L
K T R E S G T E L L A W I L G
N I S A B E P L I D S H O F F
G A B D N A H K A R O E S B E
U S A T N A N C D J B Y E R E
```

BASIN	DRUM	KEG
BASKET	FLOWERPOT	LOCKER
BATH	GLASS	POUCH
BOWL	GOBLET	SAUCEPAN
BOX	HAMPER	STEIN
BRIEFCASE	HANDBAG	TRAY
CUP	HAVERSACK	VESSEL
DISH	JUG	WALLET

SUDOKU

	4		5	8			7	
					7	9		
	1						8	
3	5			9				
1	2		8		6		9	3
				1			4	6
	3						6	
		5	1					
	8			7	5		2	

	9		3			1	5	
	3					7	6	
		2	4	6				
		9			3			
8		1				5		3
			7			8		
				3	6	4		
	8	4					3	
	1	6			7		8	

CROSSWORD

Across

1 Hardly macho
6 Deceive, trick
11 "Exodus" costar Sal
12 Marla's predecessor
13 Tiny
14 Johnny ___, "Key Largo" gangster
15 Schindler of "Schindler's List"
17 The Pointer Sisters' "___ So Shy"
18 Space
20 "My Fair Lady" character
22 Service station feature, briefly: hyph.
24 Algerian port
27 Paints unskillfully
28 Pulitzer Prize-winning columnist Mike
29 Geometric shape
30 Certain terrier, informally
31 Annually: 2 wds.
33 Opposite of a ques.
34 Michigan's biggest city: abbr.
36 Lacking imagination
38 Vinegar: prefix
40 Prussian lancer
43 Drew straight lines
44 "The Neon Bible" author
45 Psychic Edgar
46 Strange

Down

1 Fr. title
2 Crude material
3 Sadly
4 Six, in San Jose
5 City in southeastern New York
6 Wispy clouds
7 Lacto-___ vegetarian
8 12th president: 2 wds.
9 Suffix with depend or differ
10 Ancient Greek temple
16 Pub potable
18 Band with the 2014 album "Rock or Bust"
19 Jack narrowly beat him in the 1980 U.S. Open
21 Chaotic places
23 Bride's passé promise
25 In the same family tree
26 Votes against
28 Send another way
30 Armed conflict
32 Lyric poem written in couplets
34 Jeanne ___, French heroine
35 Guayaquil's country, briefly
37 Loafer or slipper
39 Gumshoe, for short
41 Boxer who often sparred verbally with Howard Cosell
42 French word for "born," seen before a maiden name

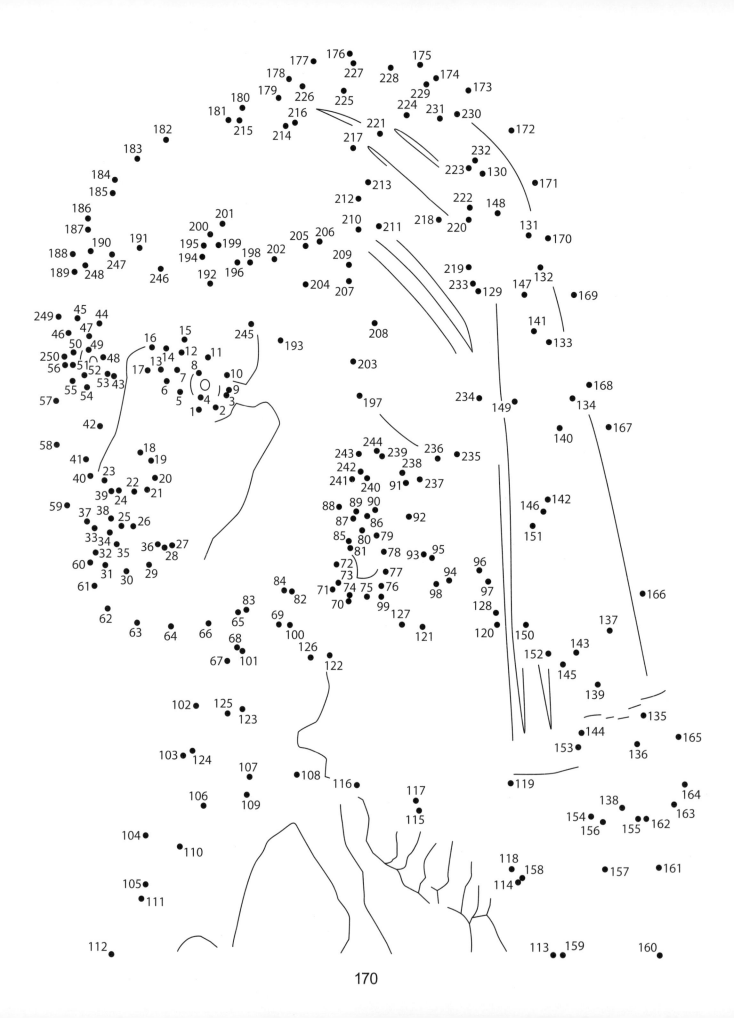

WORD SEARCH
TOOLS

```
J R E V A E L C L A V W F Q Y
A F G F Q K E Y H O L E S A W
U J U L S D P I N C E R S L H
G L O U P P L Q E L S C J E A
E M G S H E A R S K P S Q W C
R E P P O H C N E U A K M O K
B E N A L P S F N T G R F R S
A F L Z I Q M C L E B O Y T A
N T Y L Z S H L Z Z R C Y A W
D X R G O C I S P R A Y E R H
S I Q W I R E C U T T E R S Y
A I T Z D A E I J L O D E M B
W Z W Q E P S R R O T A T O R
S I C K L E M E R A U Q S T B
A F V G K R G U I D M P I P Q
```

AUGER	HAYRAKE	SCRAPER
BAND SAW	KEYHOLE SAW	SHEARS
CHOPPER	PINCERS	SICKLE
CLEAVER	PLANE	SPANNER
CORKSCREW	PUNCH	SPRAYER
DRILL	ROLLER	T SQUARE
GOUGE	ROTATOR	TROWEL
HACKSAW	SCALPEL	WIRE CUTTERS

SUDOKU

3			7		2			9
	1		6		5		3	
		6		9		1		
2		8				3		1
	6						8	
5		4				2		6
		9		2		6		
	7		8		1		4	
1			9		4			5

1			9	1	5			8	2
	1	4						3	5
				3					
			4			2		6	
		2				4			
4		8			6				
			4						
7	2						4	3	
5	6			7	3	8			

CROSSWORD

Across

1 Princely title

4 Weapon fired from a plane, initially

7 Musical syllables

10 Zidovudine, familiarly

11 Wall St. action

12 Dadaism cofounder

13 Sully

14 Some shaving cream

15 ___ la-la

16 Samuel's mentor

17 Person who takes on another's child

19 Highly concentrated

21 Palindromic boat

22 Spaghetti sauce brand

23 Informer, slangily

24 More ribald

26 Brother and husband of Isis

28 Sluggers' stats

31 Like most casseroles

32 Coating for ribs

33 Horizontal plant stem with shoots above and roots below

35 "Friends" actress Courteney

36 Fleming or Somerhalder

37 Nintendo system

38 Chivalrous guy: abbr.

39 "___ tu" (aria for Renato)

40 Lodge member

41 Story

42 "___ in November": 2 wds.

43 P.V. Narasimha ___, 1990s Indian P.M.

44 Type of medical treatment, intially

Down

1 For mature audiences: 2 wds.

2 Common shrub

3 Skimpy suits: 2 wds.

4 Primitive plants

5 In the sack

6 Father Damien's island

7 Silent film comic actor Roscoe: 2 wds.

8 Unpaid debt

9 Charles Schulz's nickname

18 Sandwich chain

20 Ray of PBS's "NewsHour"

23 Bank investments, initially

25 Man who has lost his wife by death

26 Late-night name

27 "The English Patient" setting

29 Classic, as an image

30 Group of six

32 Watch maker

34 Leon Uris's "___ 18"

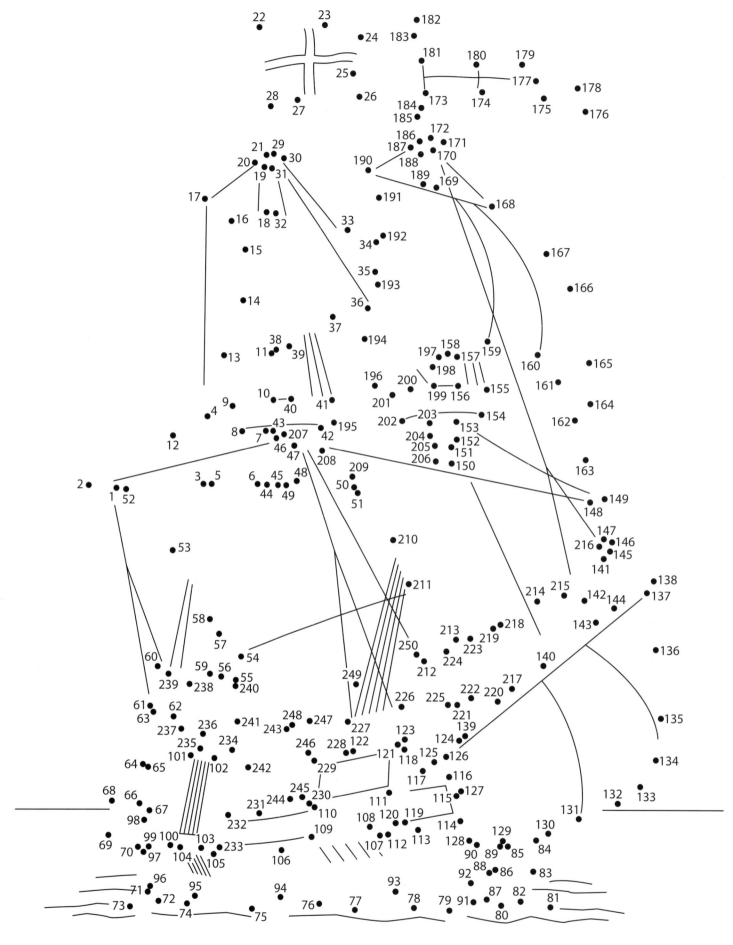

174

WORD SEARCH
CARTOON CHARACTERS

```
T N O S P M I S A S I L Z E W
P O Q U X Y N M R Q E X I H X
A K M P M P W I E O T U L P Y
H O M E B L O O N A K R G Z D
O P A R A E R P N E J E W E S
M S B M T A B Y E S Y G O E C
E D M A M H E H P Y O G M F O
R O M N A P I C R O E I O L O
S N A T N A L G F P O T B T B
I A B J E R R Y A S U N R S Y
M T K C F E A U Z S P E S I D
P E O C E Q H B A M B I S V O
S L I V L I C Y R L I Y K A O
O L S T I M P Y I L Q X V E C
N O E L X E F D M F P N Y B Z
```

BAMBI

BAMM-BAMM

BATMAN

BEAVIS

CHARLIE
  BROWN

DILBERT

DONATELLO

FELIX

GOOFY

HOMER
  SIMPSON

JERRY

LISA SIMPSON

MOWGLI

PLUTO

POPEYE

RAPHAEL

SCOOBY DOO

SNOOPY

SNOWY

SPIKE

STIMPY

SUPERMAN

TIGGER

TOM

SUDOKU

5		7				9		6
2	8			1			3	5
		2	5		7	3		
4								7
		5	4		8	1		
7	2			5			1	9
3		9				4		8

					7	3		
5	9			1				
6							2	
		7			3		1	
1	4			6			3	2
	5		4			8		
	8							5
				2			6	1
		4	9					

CROSSWORD

Across

1 Narrow path beside a road
5 ___ good turn (helps out): 2 wds.
10 In a muddle
11 Small inflatable boat
12 Dept. of Defense branch
13 Certain sorority women
14 Former Israeli P.M. Golda
15 Provide with a new supply of missiles
16 East German secret police
18 Bozo
20 Film rating org.
22 Mauna ___ (Hawaiian volcano)
23 Law's partner
26 Osprey's gripper
28 Help wanted ad letters
29 ___ Spin (classic toy): 2 wds.
31 Asinine
33 Try to corner the market on: 2 wds.
36 Girl rescued by Don Juan
38 ___ B'rith (Jewish organization)
40 "Star Wars" character ___ Binks: 2 wds.
41 Spanish eyes
42 Numbskulls
43 Depression
44 Embryo's successor
45 Primeval giant of Norse mythology

Down

1 Emerald City's creator
2 Slalom courses
3 Pay up
4 Art of knotting cord in patterns
5 Kind of store
6 Early year: 2 wds.
7 Chinese-style snack: 2 wds.
8 Hair care product
9 Affirmative votes: var.
11 Mother of Meghan, Duchess of Sussex
17 Blooming seasons, in short
19 Suffix with Jacob
21 Alaskan island
23 U.K. reference set
24 Melodic embellishment
25 Mark for misconduct
27 No one in particular
30 Bridge beams: hyph.
32 Theater name
34 Remove (as a blockage)
35 Philadelphia suburb on the Main Line
37 Back muscles, to a personal trainer
39 Elbe feeder
40 Peter Pan rival

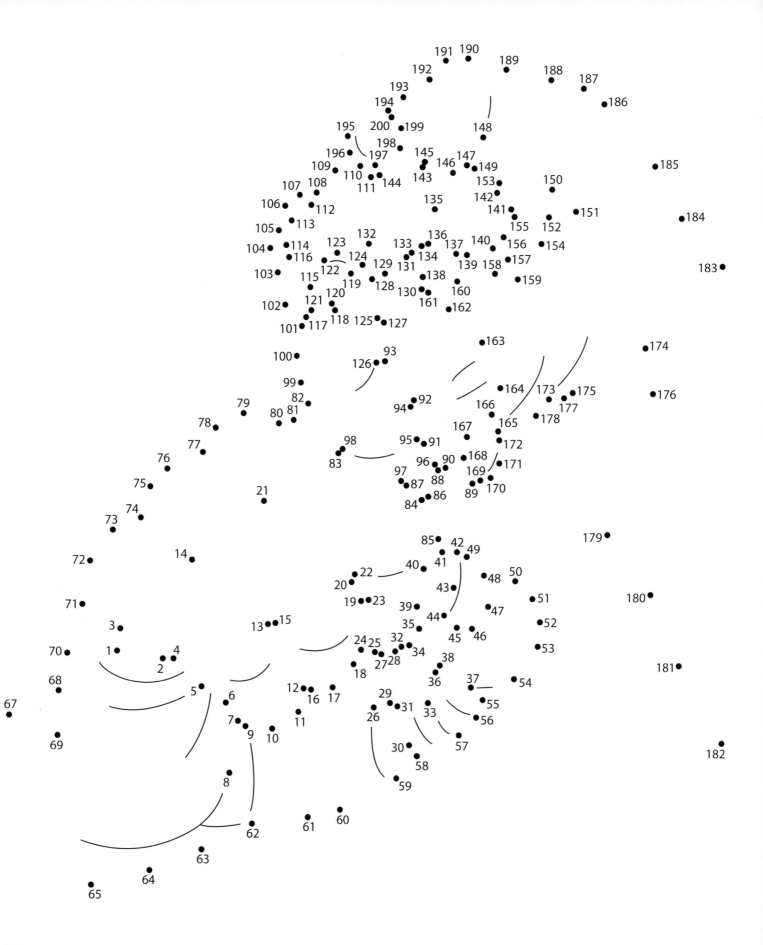

WORD SEARCH
WATERFALLS

```
B A P G K I K V G T E Z M A K
R R L C C W A Z F N U F B N M
A A E Y O U K L W I R G G C W
N G G D R Z K O L R T H E R L
D A N E K M R O E I E Z I L P
Y I A T C B D N L W B M R N A
W N U T I G O R D A W M L O E
I F O I L H W H Z A H G U O Y
N I M F S V I C T O R I A Y T
E X J O R E G S K R I M M L X
D G H S T C O U S A V A H U L
D S V S R N G Z G R J J H D Z
A K N I R G A P I N G G I L L
N U O T E P O H I G U A S S U
O Z A M W Y A O P J K X M B D
```

ANGEL	HOPETOUN	SLICK ROCK
BRANDYWINE	IGUASSU	TOLMER
BROWNE	KRIMML	TUGELA
DETTIFOSS	NIAGARA	UTIGORD
FITZROY	PHANTOM	VICTORIA
GAPING GILL	RHINE	WATSON
HALOKU	RINKA	WINDOW
HAVASU	SHOSHONE	YUMBILLA

SUDOKU

8	9			7			1	3
		6				5		
7			4		8			6
	4			8			3	
			5		6			
	8			1			4	
2			9		4			7
		4				1		
9	6			3			2	4

	9		1				5	2
3		8					9	
1			9			6		
			4					5
		7				4		
2					1			
		1			2			7
	6					8		9
7	5				6		3	

CROSSWORD

Across

1 Acrimonious
7 Gadget with lots of numbers on it
11 Comment from the defeated: 2 wds.
12 "Et voilà!": hyph.
13 Rice dish made with saffron
14 Contemptible sort, slangily
15 Letters on some pumps
16 Molten rock
17 1980s TV E.T.
19 Normandy invasion start: hyph.
21 Never, in Berlin
22 Look for again
26 ___ Lingus (Irish airline)
27 Doubly
28 Married mujer: abbr.
29 Submerged (as a shipwreck)
31 Slammer
32 Chase of "Now, Voyager"
34 Delivery room doctors, for short
35 Nero's successor
38 How-___ (guides)
40 Medley
41 Garments worn in ancient Rome
44 Till section
45 Hardly a brainiac
46 Keystone structure
47 Straighten out

Down

1 Marcel Marceau character
2 "I like ___ lot!": 2 wds.
3 Palmlike plant: 2 wds.
4 Mosaic piece
5 Went sniggling
6 Nutritional std.
7 "___ that" (the text runs thus): 2 wds.
8 Qualm
9 One-time Tampa Bay Buccaneers tackle Jason
10 Disk information
16 Actresses Marsh and West
17 Anthologies (suffix)
18 Place
20 Tea or coffee, e.g.
23 "Do the Right Thing" actor Giancarlo
24 Jewish holiday eve
25 It lies between Neb. and Okla.
27 First name in horror
30 Prevent from happening, slangily
33 "___ in the South" (V. S. Naipaul travelogue): 2 wds.
35 "I've ___ Feeling" (Beatles song): 2 wds.
36 Yankee or Angel, for short
37 Member of "The Mod Squad"
39 Ten sawbucks: 2 wds.
41 Ft. Worth college
42 102, in old Rome
43 NBC sketch series

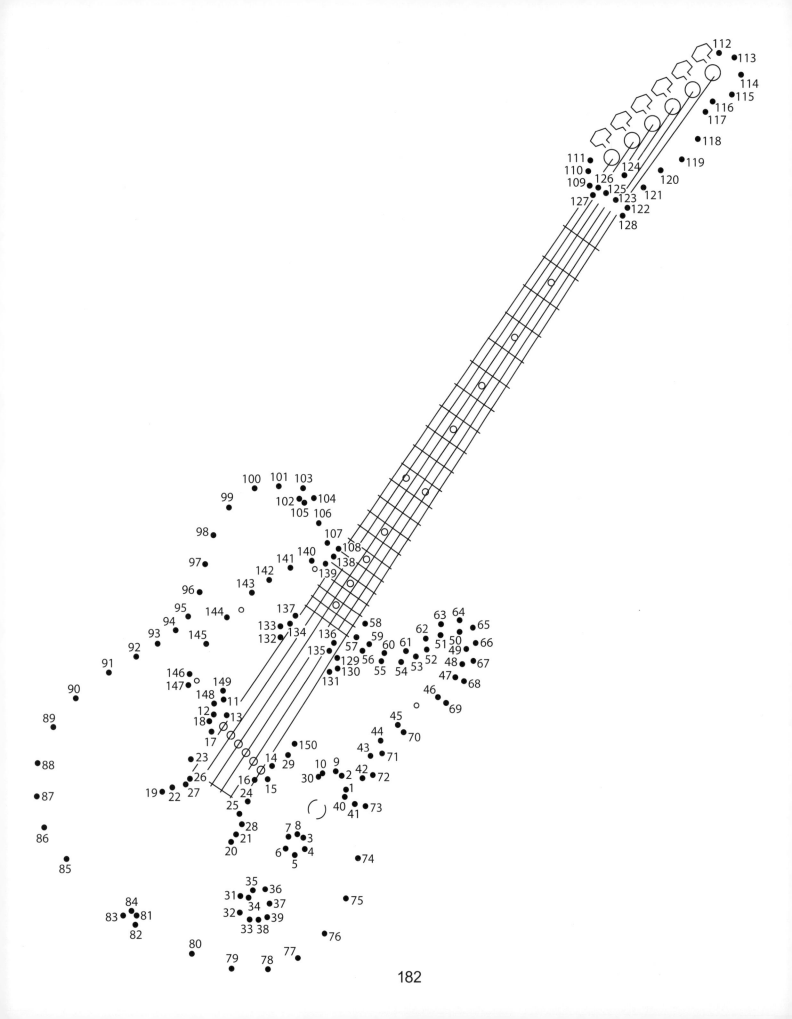

WORD SEARCH
FRUITS

```
P P T I U R F N O I S S A P T
I R L R O S A O F S T C K F A
M U L P L G S M C L N F E F U
T N U T U J U E X I A I E L Q
P E A A F D W L Y R R E H C M
U M V R K R A O L A R T B K U
M A E E C H O O H Y U G L I K
P O L S F W G M B Y C W F I B
K L P E A N Z X A E K H B U D
I E P D A T E J G D C S E E Y
N M A M F D S N F T A I L E M
T O C I R P A U F A L W A O N
F P U E R R A R M D B I M X E
I J A V O C A D O A U K M Q F
G T P A D A O O C P Z Q C E P
```

AKEE	GUAVA	PASSION FRUIT
APPLE	KIWI	PLUM
APRICOT	KUMQUAT	POMELO
AVOCADO	LEMON	PRUNE
BLACK CURRANT	LIME	PUMPKIN
CHERRY	LYCHEE	SATSUMA
DATE	MANGO	SLOE
FIG	ORANGE	UGLI

SUDOKU

			5	9			8	
8	7	3		4				5
			7					6
		9					8	
1		2				6		7
	4					9		
4					1			
5				6		3	1	9
9			8	2				

	8		2	1				
5							9	1
6			5				3	7
			9				4	
	3	4				5	7	
	6				5			
3	1				9			4
4	2							5
				5	1		2	

CROSSWORD

Across

1 Eastwood in Rawhide
6 "___ Yellow Ribbon Round the Ole Oak Tree" (song): 2 wds.
10 Remove one's headgear
11 Mountain range in western Russia
12 They're played indoors: 2 wds.
14 Mahmoud Abbas's grp.
15 Stephen of "Still Crazy"
16 New Deal prog.
17 Sodium chloride atom
18 Producer: abbr.
19 Brit. lexicon
20 Bavarian river
22 Title for a British prime minister, briefly: 2 wds.
24 Have ___ (drink ale): 2 wds.
26 Seed coverings
28 Real: Ger.
32 First of a Latin trio
33 "___ Love You So" (song in the movie "Cocktail"): 2 wds.
35 "___ of little faith…": 2 wds.
36 Twin killings, in baseball, initially
37 Big name in IT
38 C.E.O.'s degree, often
39 Places to find paper and pens: 2 wds.
42 One of the Horae
43 Military V.I.P., slangily
44 Where a bird sleeps
45 Dominant 1980s tennis player

Down

1 Modern affluent sort (acronym)
2 Watch type
3 Seat of power
4 One-time domestic flight co.
5 Eye site
6 La-la lead-in
7 "You are not!" retort: 3 wds.
8 "Ocean's ___"
9 Syria's Hafez-al-___
11 Lorre's part in "Casablanca"
13 Short course for updating previous training
21 Thor Heyerdahl craft: 2 wds.
23 Charlemagne's realm, shortly
25 Flaxen-haired
26 Unit of electric current
27 Characters in "Macbeth" and "Richard II"
29 "Now, seriously!": 2 wds.
30 Mule, for one
31 Thistlelike plant
32 Contribute to the mix: 2 wds.
34 Poker player's announcement: 2 wds.
40 Chess piece, briefly
41 Heartache

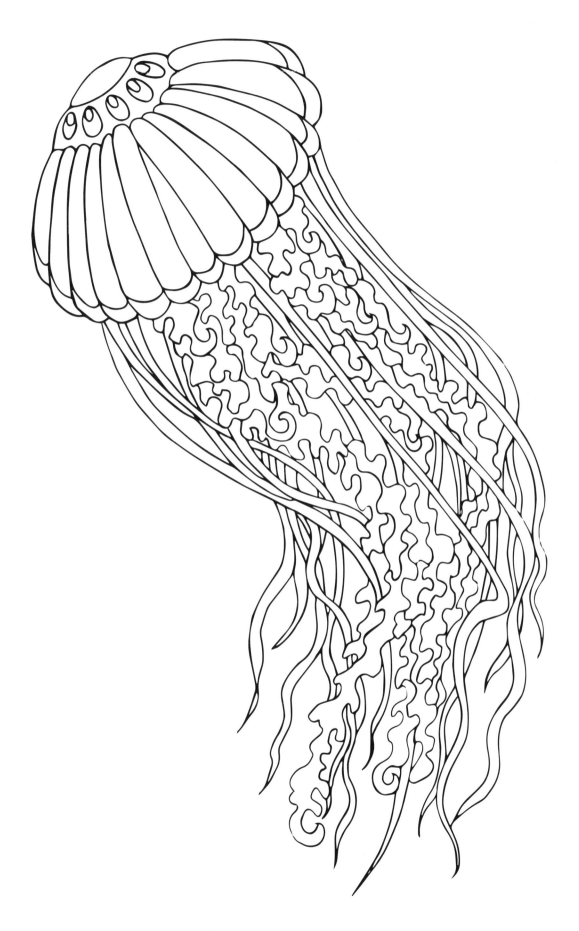

SOLUTIONS

Page 7

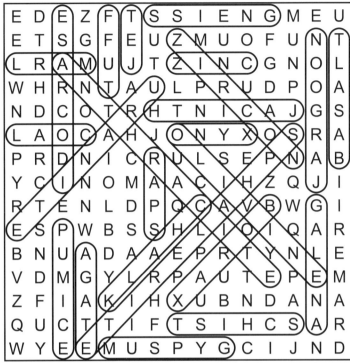

Page 8

1	2	7	6	8	9	4	5	3
6	4	8	5	2	3	1	7	9
3	9	5	7	4	1	8	2	6
2	7	3	4	1	5	9	6	8
4	6	1	8	9	7	5	3	2
5	8	9	2	3	6	7	1	4
8	3	6	1	7	4	2	9	5
9	1	4	3	5	2	6	8	7
7	5	2	9	6	8	3	4	1

7	6	3	8	5	9	2	4	1
8	4	9	6	2	1	5	3	7
1	5	2	7	4	3	8	9	6
3	2	6	1	7	4	9	8	5
5	1	8	9	6	2	3	7	4
4	9	7	3	8	5	6	1	2
6	8	5	4	3	7	1	2	9
9	3	4	2	1	6	7	5	8
2	7	1	5	9	8	4	6	3

Page 9

P	L	A	N	■	S	P	E	C	I	E
D	E	C	O	■	N	I	P	P	O	N
F	A	R	R	E	A	C	H	I	N	G
S	N	O	W	L	I	N	E	■		
			■	S	L	I	M	I	E	R
L	O	N	G	A	■	C	E	L	L	O
I	C	E	E	■		R	E	B	A	
R	H	E	T	T	■	L	A	R	A	M
A	S	T	A	R	T	E	■			
		■	N	O	O	N	T	I	D	E
Z	I	G	G	Y	M	A	R	L	E	Y
A	D	O	R	E	E	■	I	Y	A	R
P	A	P	Y	R	I	■	B	A	R	E

Page 10

TIGER

Page 11

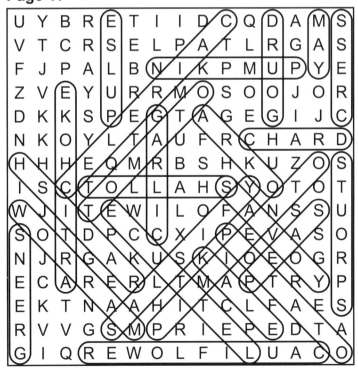

Page 12

4	3	5	6	8	9	7	1	2
8	2	6	5	1	7	3	4	9
7	1	9	3	4	2	5	6	8
9	8	2	1	7	3	4	5	6
1	4	7	2	5	6	8	9	3
5	6	3	8	9	4	1	2	7
3	5	4	9	2	8	6	7	1
6	9	1	7	3	5	2	8	4
2	7	8	4	6	1	9	3	5

8	4	5	6	9	7	1	2	3
6	2	3	8	1	4	5	7	9
1	7	9	2	3	5	6	8	4
4	8	2	3	6	1	7	9	5
7	3	1	5	8	9	4	6	2
5	9	6	4	7	2	8	3	1
2	5	8	9	4	6	3	1	7
9	6	7	1	5	3	2	4	8
3	1	4	7	2	8	9	5	6

Page 13

D	A	S	■	S	N	A	■	I	A	L
E	C	O	■	O	O	H	■	C	T	A
S	E	M	I	P	R	O	■	E	T	C
C	H	E	S	H	I	R	E	C	A	T
■		L	A	I	■	S	S	R		■
C	E	I	B	A	■	E	P	E	E	S
P	O	K	E	■	■		O	A	R	S
L	E	E	L	A	■	C	U	M	I	N
■		I	L	L	■	A	S	S		■
P	O	T	A	T	O	S	A	C	K	S
H	R	H	■	I	M	P	L	O	R	E
O	D	O	■	M	A	A	■	O	O	N
S	O	T	■	A	R	R	■	P	C	S

Page 14

DISCUS THROWER

233

SOLUTIONS

Page 15

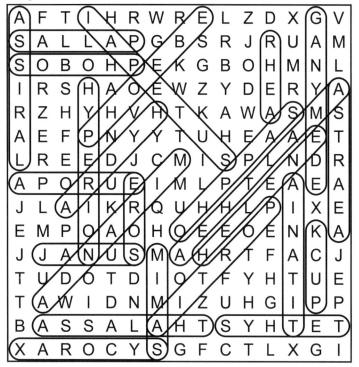

Page 16

2	1	9	7	8	4	3	6	5
6	4	3	5	2	9	1	8	7
7	5	8	1	6	3	2	9	4
5	3	2	6	9	1	7	4	8
1	7	4	3	5	8	6	2	9
8	9	6	2	4	7	5	1	3
9	2	1	8	7	5	4	3	6
4	6	7	9	3	2	8	5	1
3	8	5	4	1	6	9	7	2

6	1	2	4	5	8	3	9	7
3	7	5	1	9	2	4	8	6
9	8	4	3	7	6	1	5	2
2	9	8	6	1	7	5	4	3
7	3	6	5	8	4	9	2	1
4	5	1	2	3	9	7	6	8
5	2	7	9	6	3	8	1	4
8	6	9	7	4	1	2	3	5
1	4	3	8	2	5	6	7	9

Page 17

W	O	E	S	■	O	B	T	U	S	E
S	H	A	K	■	M	I	A	M	I	S
J	O	V	I	■	O	A	X	A	C	A
■	■	E	N	R	O	L	L	■	■	■
■	E	S	N	E	■	Y	A	B	B	A
D	I	D	Y	A	■	S	W	O	R	N
A	G	R	■	■	■	■	N	U	I	■
T	H	O	R	S	■	A	D	V	I	L
S	T	P	A	T	■	P	E	O	N	■
■	■	■	G	A	I	E	T	Y	■	■
R	O	O	M	B	A	■	A	A	R	P
O	N	L	O	A	N	■	I	G	O	R
C	O	A	P	T	S	■	N	E	B	O

Page 18

DAFFODIL

Page 19

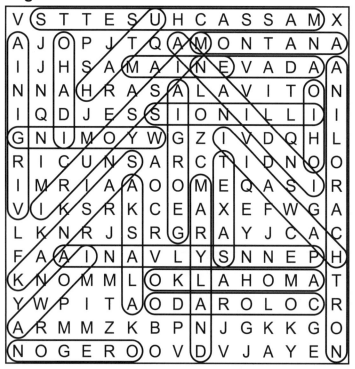

Page 20

5	8	1	3	6	4	7	2	9
4	3	9	2	7	1	5	8	6
7	2	6	9	5	8	1	4	3
1	5	8	7	9	6	2	3	4
2	9	4	1	3	5	6	7	8
6	7	3	4	8	2	9	5	1
9	1	5	8	2	3	4	6	7
8	6	7	5	4	9	3	1	2
3	4	2	6	1	7	8	9	5

2	1	6	9	3	5	4	7	8
8	4	3	7	2	6	9	5	1
5	9	7	1	4	8	3	6	2
7	6	4	8	1	2	5	9	3
9	2	5	6	7	3	8	1	4
1	3	8	5	9	4	6	2	7
6	5	2	4	8	1	7	3	9
3	8	9	2	6	7	1	4	5
4	7	1	3	5	9	2	8	6

Page 21

N	I	M	B	U	S	■	S	A	T	B
G	R	I	L	L	E	■	C	B	E	R
O	R	I	A	N	A	■	H	A	R	A
■	■	■	N	A	R	C	O	T	I	C
R	I	S	K	■	S	H	O	■	■	■
A	K	E	E	M	■	A	L	U	L	A
P	E	E	T	E	■	L	T	G	E	N
A	S	S	Y	R	■	K	E	L	S	O
■	■	■	B	C	E	■	A	I	T	S
P	R	O	L	I	F	I	C	■	■	■
R	I	T	A	■	L	A	H	O	R	E
I	C	O	N	■	A	G	E	G	A	P
M	A	S	K	■	T	O	R	S	O	S

Page 22

CAT

234

SOLUTIONS

Page 23

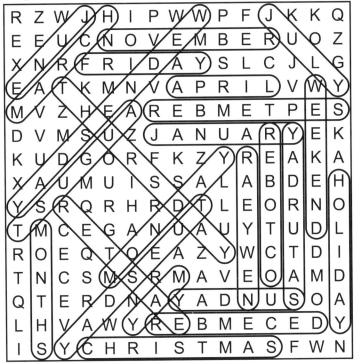

Page 24

9	6	3	7	1	2	4	5	8
7	4	8	6	5	3	1	2	9
5	2	1	8	4	9	7	6	3
3	9	5	1	8	6	2	4	7
6	8	4	9	2	7	5	3	1
2	1	7	5	3	4	9	8	6
8	3	9	4	7	5	6	1	2
1	5	6	2	9	8	3	7	4
4	7	2	3	6	1	8	9	5

7	4	8	3	1	9	6	2	5
2	9	5	8	6	7	4	3	1
6	3	1	2	4	5	8	7	9
3	1	2	6	7	4	9	5	8
9	6	4	5	8	3	2	1	7
8	5	7	9	2	1	3	4	6
4	8	9	1	5	2	7	6	3
5	7	3	4	9	6	1	8	2
1	2	6	7	3	8	5	9	4

Page 25

W	A	S	P	■	■	O	X	I	D	E
O	J	A	I	■	S	P	O	O	R	S
L	A	M	P	■	P	E	L	L	E	T
F	R	A	P	P	E	■	O	E	D	S
■	■	■	D	I	R	E	C	T	■	■
I	T	A	■	I	D	O	L	I	Z	E
T	A	M	■	M	D	S	■	N	E	S
Y	E	S	M	A	A	M	■	N	E	C
■	■	■	U	L	T	I	M	O	■	■
S	L	U	T	■	I	C	I	C	L	E
T	O	P	T	E	N	■	N	E	E	R
R	A	T	E	D	G	■	E	N	C	O
S	M	O	R	E	■	■	O	T	H	O

Page 26

SAILING YACHT

Page 27

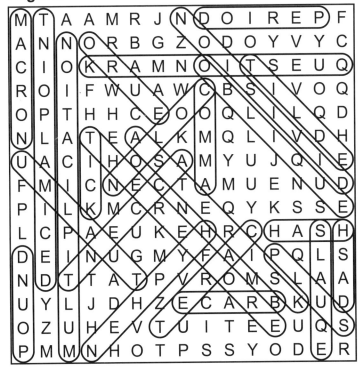

Page 28

6	3	1	8	5	4	2	7	9
2	5	7	9	1	6	3	4	8
8	9	4	2	3	7	1	5	6
5	7	8	4	2	3	9	6	1
3	6	2	7	9	1	4	8	5
4	1	9	6	8	5	7	2	3
1	8	6	3	7	2	5	9	4
7	4	5	1	6	9	8	3	2
9	2	3	5	4	8	6	1	7

4	5	3	9	2	7	8	1	6
1	2	6	8	4	3	5	9	7
8	7	9	1	6	5	3	2	4
2	3	5	4	1	8	7	6	9
9	8	4	6	7	2	1	3	5
7	6	1	5	3	9	2	4	8
3	4	7	2	8	6	9	5	1
5	1	8	3	9	4	6	7	2
6	9	2	7	5	1	4	8	3

Page 29

P	E	S	T	■	■	K	O	J	A	K
R	A	H	A	L	■	E	D	U	C	E
S	T	O	L	I	■	Y	E	N	T	E
■	■	W	E	N	C	H	■	I	I	N
C	E	O	■	C	U	O	M	O	■	■
A	M	F	M	■	B	L	U	R	R	Y
L	I	S	A	S	■	E	L	V	E	S
F	L	U	N	K	Y	■	L	A	Z	E
■	■	P	E	A	R	L	■	R	A	R
P	C	P	■	L	S	A	T	S	■	■
A	L	O	A	D	■	S	H	I	R	R
G	A	R	N	I	■	■	S	E	T	O	N
O	P	T	I	C	■	■	O	Y	E	S

Page 30

SPARROW

SOLUTIONS

Page 31

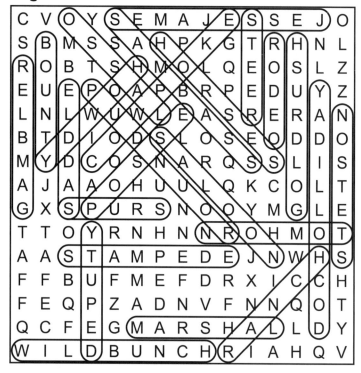

Page 32

7	1	2	8	5	6	3	9	4
6	8	4	3	1	9	5	2	7
3	5	9	7	2	4	6	8	1
1	7	5	4	3	2	8	6	9
2	3	6	9	8	7	4	1	5
9	4	8	5	6	1	7	3	2
4	9	1	6	7	8	2	5	3
5	6	7	2	9	3	1	4	8
8	2	3	1	4	5	9	7	6

7	6	5	2	9	1	8	3	4
1	4	9	3	7	8	6	5	2
8	2	3	4	6	5	7	1	9
5	3	6	9	8	7	2	4	1
9	8	4	6	1	2	3	7	5
2	7	1	5	4	3	9	6	8
4	5	8	7	2	6	1	9	3
6	9	2	1	3	4	5	8	7
3	1	7	8	5	9	4	2	6

Page 33

I	N	P	U	T		P	I	Q	U	E
N	E	A	L	E		A	L	U	L	A
B	U	T	T	E		D	E	A	N	S
O	T	E		N	E	L		D	A	T
A	R	R		S	N	O		R	E	S
R	O	F	L		A	C	T	I		
D	N	A	S	E		K	A	P	P	A
		M	U	L	L		B	A	I	T
B	M	I		N	A	L		R	E	A
I	A	L		I	A	T		T	R	L
O	N	I	O	N		G	E	I	C	O
T	E	A	M	O		E	S	T	E	S
A	S	S	E	S		N	E	E	D	S

Page 34

TREE FROG

Page 35

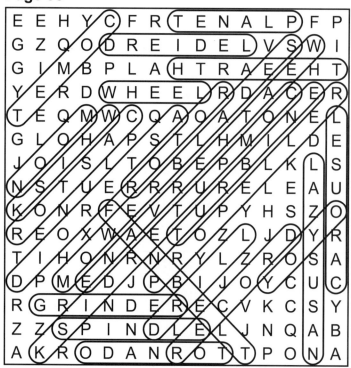

Page 36

2	5	9	3	6	4	8	7	1
7	4	3	1	5	8	6	9	2
8	1	6	9	7	2	5	3	4
6	8	5	4	3	1	7	2	9
9	7	4	2	8	5	1	6	3
1	3	2	6	9	7	4	5	8
5	2	7	8	4	3	9	1	6
4	9	1	5	2	6	3	8	7
3	6	8	7	1	9	2	4	5

5	9	7	4	6	8	2	1	3
4	3	2	1	5	9	6	8	7
8	1	6	2	3	7	4	5	9
3	4	8	7	9	1	5	6	2
6	7	5	3	8	2	1	9	4
1	2	9	6	4	5	3	7	8
7	8	1	5	2	4	9	3	6
9	6	4	8	1	3	7	2	5
2	5	3	9	7	6	8	4	1

Page 37

C	R	I	B		S	A	F	E	C	O
C	H	A	I		S	T	O	R	R	S
C	E	N	T	R	I	F	U	G	A	L
P	A	S	T	A			L	O	G	O
			E	R	I	T	U			
C	O	E	N		W	I	P	E	U	P
U	R	L		B	I	D		L	R	G
R	U	M	P	U	S		M	I	N	S
			U	T	H	E	R			
P	R	O	F		S	T	E	E	D	
E	I	F	F	E	L	T	O	W	E	R
P	L	A	I	N	T		A	E	R	Y
S	E	N	N	A	S		D	S	O	S

Page 38

MODEL T

SOLUTIONS

Page 39

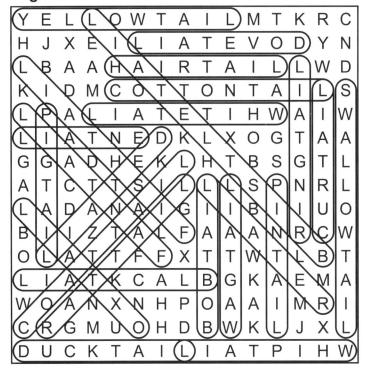

Page 40

5	8	9	4	3	6	2	7	1
2	6	7	8	5	1	4	3	9
1	4	3	2	7	9	6	5	8
7	1	4	6	9	2	5	8	3
9	5	2	3	8	7	1	4	6
8	3	6	5	1	4	7	9	2
3	2	8	7	6	5	9	1	4
6	9	5	1	4	8	3	2	7
4	7	1	9	2	3	8	6	5

8	1	6	5	3	4	9	2	7
9	7	4	1	2	8	5	6	3
2	3	5	9	6	7	8	1	4
1	8	7	4	9	3	6	5	2
4	6	2	7	1	5	3	9	8
5	9	3	2	8	6	7	4	1
6	4	1	3	7	9	2	8	5
7	5	8	6	4	2	1	3	9
3	2	9	8	5	1	4	7	6

Page 41

Page 42

VAN GOGH

Page 43

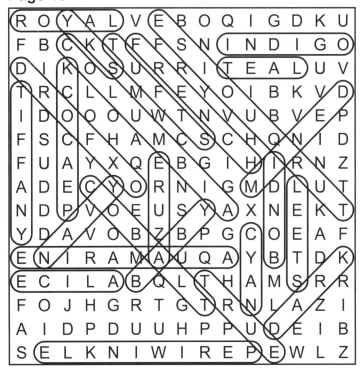

Page 44

4	5	1	3	7	6	2	9	8
9	8	3	2	4	1	7	5	6
7	2	6	5	9	8	4	1	3
2	1	4	6	5	9	3	8	7
6	3	5	4	8	7	1	2	9
8	7	9	1	2	3	6	4	5
1	4	7	8	6	5	9	3	2
5	6	2	9	3	4	8	7	1
3	9	8	7	1	2	5	6	4

2	8	7	1	9	6	5	3	4
5	6	9	2	3	4	1	7	8
1	3	4	7	8	5	2	6	9
8	9	1	4	7	2	3	5	6
3	7	6	8	5	1	4	9	2
4	5	2	3	6	9	7	8	1
6	2	8	5	4	7	9	1	3
9	1	5	6	2	3	8	4	7
7	4	3	9	1	8	6	2	5

Page 45

	D	R	A	P	E	D		F	I	G
A	C	E	T	O	N	E		R	S	A
B	A	M	B	O	O	S	H	O	O	T
A	R	O	A	R		C	O	S	M	O
S	E	T	T			E	R	T	E	S
H	A	E		P	O	N	D	E	R	
		C	R	O	W	D	E	D		
	D	O	A	L	L	S		F	O	B
S	E	N	N	A			F	L	U	E
A	F	T	E	R		M	I	A	T	A
F	I	R	E	C	R	A	C	K	E	R
E	L	O		A	I	R	H	E	A	D
S	E	L		P	A	L	E	S	T	

Page 46

STATUE OF LIBERTY

SOLUTIONS

Page 47

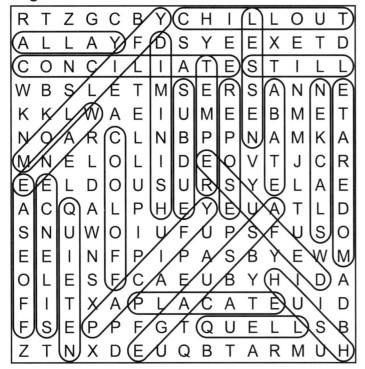

Page 48

7	9	6	3	5	4	1	2	8
5	1	3	8	2	9	4	7	6
8	4	2	1	6	7	9	3	5
1	5	8	4	7	3	6	9	2
2	3	4	9	1	6	5	8	7
6	7	9	2	8	5	3	4	1
9	2	5	7	3	1	8	6	4
4	8	1	6	9	2	7	5	3
3	6	7	5	4	8	2	1	9

2	9	3	5	6	8	1	4	7
4	8	1	3	2	7	9	6	5
6	7	5	1	9	4	3	2	8
7	5	4	2	3	1	6	8	9
1	3	8	6	4	9	5	7	2
9	6	2	7	8	5	4	1	3
5	4	6	9	7	2	8	3	1
8	2	9	4	1	3	7	5	6
3	1	7	8	5	6	2	9	4

Page 49

C	O	L	L	A	R	■	A	B	R	I
O	T	I	O	S	E	■	R	I	A	L
R	E	L	U	C	T	A	N	T	L	Y
■	■	T	O	R	C	■	T	E	A	■
A	R	I	S	T	O	T	L	E	■	■
L	O	T	■	■	G	E	O	R	G	E
M	U	S	T	A	R	D	S	E	E	D
S	E	A	B	E	E	■	N	E	D	■
■	■	C	A	S	S	A	N	D	R	A
S	R	I	■	I	S	M	E	■	■	■
C	O	N	T	R	I	B	U	T	E	S
A	B	C	D	■	■	V	E	R	I	T	Y
M	O	H	S	■	E	R	O	D	E	R

Page 50

TEDDY BEAR

Page 51

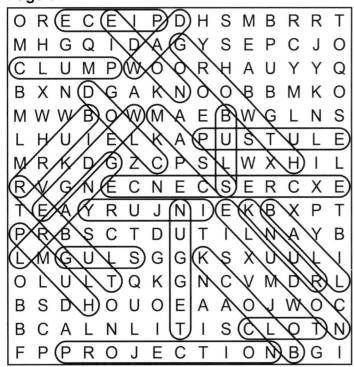

Page 52

5	3	1	6	7	2	9	8	4
8	7	6	1	9	4	3	2	5
2	4	9	8	5	3	1	6	7
9	1	8	7	4	6	2	5	3
6	2	7	3	8	5	4	9	1
3	5	4	9	2	1	8	7	6
4	8	5	2	1	7	6	3	9
1	9	3	5	6	8	7	4	2
7	6	2	4	3	9	5	1	8

9	4	3	5	2	8	6	7	1
2	5	1	7	9	6	8	4	3
8	6	7	3	1	4	9	2	5
7	1	8	9	5	3	2	6	4
4	2	5	6	8	7	3	1	9
3	9	6	1	4	2	5	8	7
1	8	2	4	3	9	7	5	6
6	3	4	2	7	5	1	9	8
5	7	9	8	6	1	4	3	2

Page 53

T	O	J	O	■	D	J	I	N	N	I
U	B	E	R	■	N	A	B	O	R	S
B	O	S	N	■	A	M	E	R	C	E
B	L	U	E	F	L	U	■	■	■	■
■	■	■	R	A	P	T	U	R	E	
O	D	D	J	O	B	■	O	S	E	S
D	E	B	U	G	■	B	R	I	A	N
O	W	L	S	■	A	R	C	A	D	E
M	Y	S	T	E	R	Y	■	■	■	■
■	■	■	R	A	N	K	I	N	G	
S	C	H	W	A	B	■	U	N	I	T
G	O	A	W	O	L	■	R	E	N	O
T	O	L	I	F	E	■	D	S	O	S

Page 54

EMPEROR MOTH

238

SOLUTIONS

Page 55

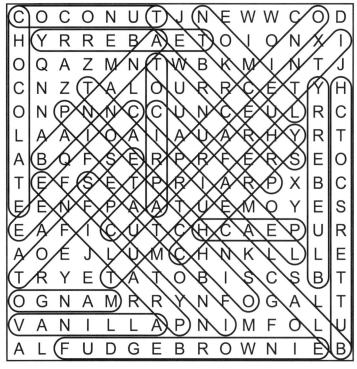

Page 56

8	1	5	7	3	9	6	4	2
7	6	9	2	4	8	1	5	3
2	4	3	5	1	6	7	9	8
1	5	4	9	7	2	8	3	6
9	7	6	4	8	3	5	2	1
3	2	8	6	5	1	4	7	9
4	8	1	3	9	7	2	6	5
6	9	7	8	2	5	3	1	4
5	3	2	1	6	4	9	8	7

3	1	8	7	9	6	2	4	5
9	5	7	2	4	8	1	3	6
4	6	2	5	3	1	9	8	7
2	7	9	1	5	4	8	6	3
5	3	6	9	8	2	7	1	4
1	8	4	6	7	3	5	2	9
8	9	1	3	6	5	4	7	2
7	4	3	8	2	9	6	5	1
6	2	5	4	1	7	3	9	8

Page 57

```
E S T D   G F O R C E
D O H A   N E W A G E
D U E L   E E N S I E
A P P E T I T E
    O T O S   R A D O
R I G H T S   S D A K
P S U         J N R
M A E S   U N C O L A
S Y S T   P U L I
    A L L I A N C E
P H O B I A   S I L K
T E F L O N   S N E E
A T T E N D   A G A S
```

Page 58

PUPPY

Page 59

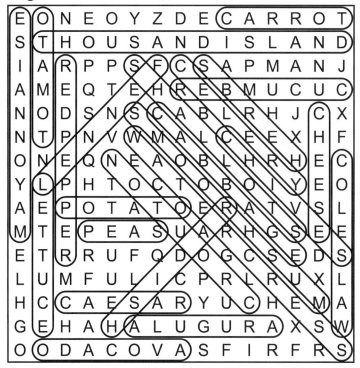

Page 60

3	7	5	6	9	1	4	2	8
6	9	2	3	4	8	7	1	5
1	8	4	5	7	2	6	9	3
5	3	6	9	1	7	2	8	4
8	4	7	2	3	6	1	5	9
2	1	9	4	8	5	3	6	7
7	5	3	1	2	9	8	4	6
4	6	1	8	5	3	9	7	2
9	2	8	7	6	4	5	3	1

8	7	9	1	6	5	4	2	3
6	5	4	7	2	3	1	9	8
3	2	1	9	8	4	6	7	5
5	1	7	8	9	6	2	3	4
4	9	3	2	5	1	7	8	6
2	8	6	4	3	7	9	5	1
1	3	5	6	7	2	8	4	9
7	4	8	3	1	9	5	6	2
9	6	2	5	4	8	3	1	7

Page 61

```
A I M A T   K R U P P
W R O T H   F E T E D
N E C K E R C H I E F
    C A M O   E L L S
I P A   A B R A
Y E S M   B U R S A R
A R I O T   T S L O T
R U N L E T   E I N E
    E L I A   P E S
S I G S   S R I S
W O R K M A N S H I P
I N A I D   E L O R A
T A U N T   L E D T O
```

Page 62

TOY RABBIT

SOLUTIONS

Page 63

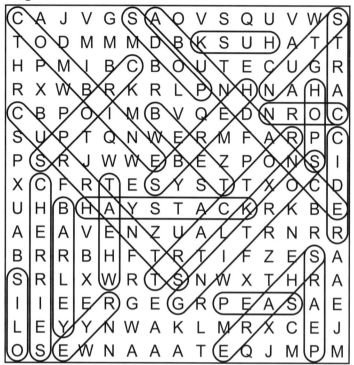

Page 64

3	1	2	6	7	4	8	5	9
6	9	4	8	2	5	1	7	3
5	8	7	9	1	3	4	6	2
8	4	9	2	6	7	5	3	1
1	6	5	3	4	8	2	9	7
2	7	3	1	5	9	6	4	8
9	2	8	4	3	6	7	1	5
7	3	6	5	8	1	9	2	4
4	5	1	7	9	2	3	8	6

2	9	4	5	1	7	8	6	3
7	3	5	9	6	8	4	2	1
1	6	8	2	4	3	7	5	9
3	8	6	1	5	9	2	7	4
5	2	9	4	7	6	3	1	8
4	7	1	3	8	2	5	9	6
8	1	2	6	3	5	9	4	7
6	5	3	7	9	4	1	8	2
9	4	7	8	2	1	6	3	5

Page 65

E	D	D	Y		M	I	K	I	T	A
L	E	O	I		O	C	U	L	A	R
H	A	W	K		R	E	W	E	T	S
I	N	N	E		O	D	A			
		G	S	O	S		I	C	O	N
M	E	R		L	E	F	T	O	F	F
A	D	A	G	E		R	I	V	A	L
H	Y	D	R	A	T	E		E	N	D
I	S	E	E		H	E	B	R		
			M	E	E		I	N	M	E
O	C	E	L	L	I		P	O	O	L
A	I	R	I	E	R		E	T	D	S
R	A	I	N	E	S		D	E	E	E

Page 66

SPITFIRE

Page 67

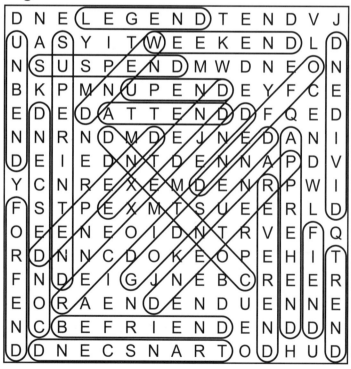

Page 68

4	2	8	3	5	9	1	7	6
6	1	9	4	2	7	8	5	3
7	5	3	8	6	1	4	9	2
3	8	4	5	9	2	6	1	7
2	6	1	7	8	3	5	4	9
5	9	7	6	1	4	2	3	8
9	3	6	1	4	8	7	2	5
8	4	2	9	7	5	3	6	1
1	7	5	2	3	6	9	8	4

9	4	7	6	3	2	1	8	5
3	2	1	8	5	7	4	6	9
5	8	6	1	9	4	2	7	3
4	1	9	3	8	5	6	2	7
8	6	2	9	7	1	5	3	4
7	5	3	4	2	6	8	9	1
1	3	8	2	4	9	7	5	6
6	9	5	7	1	8	3	4	2
2	7	4	5	6	3	9	1	8

Page 69

T	A	B	L	E		S	L	O	M	O
S	T	R	A	P		M	O	P	U	P
O	T	E	R	I		I	D	E	S	T
S	S	A		S	A	T	I	N		
		D	U	T	C	H		Y	E	W
S	A	M	P	L	E		N	O	R	A
E	R	A	S	E		L	A	U	E	R
R	A	C	Y		F	L	O	R	I	N
F	G	H		L	E	A	S	H		
		I	C	A	H	N		E	S	L
M	A	N	U	P		E	N	A	M	I
T	W	E	R	P		R	E	R	U	N
A	S	S	T	S		O	U	T	T	A

Page 70

POP ART

240

SOLUTIONS

3	5	2	1	9	7	6	8	4
6	9	7	4	3	8	2	5	1
1	8	4	5	2	6	9	3	7
5	2	6	9	4	3	1	7	8
8	7	9	6	5	1	3	4	2
4	1	3	8	7	2	5	9	6
9	6	5	2	8	4	7	1	3
2	3	8	7	1	5	4	6	9
7	4	1	3	6	9	8	2	5

8	2	5	3	6	1	4	9	7
1	3	7	2	4	9	6	5	8
6	4	9	8	5	7	3	1	2
7	8	3	6	1	4	5	2	9
9	6	2	5	3	8	7	4	1
4	5	1	7	9	2	8	6	3
2	1	6	4	8	3	9	7	5
5	9	8	1	7	6	2	3	4
3	7	4	9	2	5	1	8	6

```
E R O D E S █ █ M A T
N O N U S E █ B A L E
T O E C A P █ U R L S
O K O K █ T O N S I L
M I N I █ O S H E A █
B E E N █ K N E A D S
█ █ G R O A N █ █ █ █
P H A S E I █ B O S S
A O R T A █ U R I C █
T U M O R S █ R E G O
I D I O █ E L N I N O
N O E L █ T E E D U P
A N S █ S T R A P S █
```

SUPER HERO

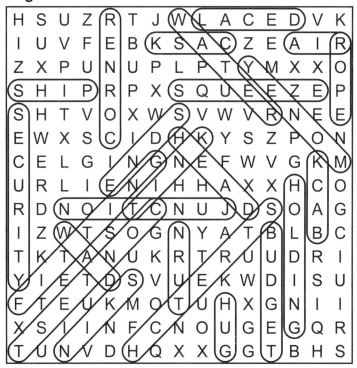

5	1	2	4	6	7	3	9	8
7	3	6	2	9	8	5	4	1
4	9	8	3	1	5	7	6	2
2	5	9	1	8	4	6	7	3
1	8	7	6	5	3	4	2	9
6	4	3	7	2	9	1	8	5
3	6	1	8	7	2	9	5	4
8	7	5	9	4	1	2	3	6
9	2	4	5	3	6	8	1	7

7	4	8	9	3	6	5	2	1
3	6	1	5	7	2	9	4	8
9	5	2	4	1	8	7	3	6
2	1	9	8	6	7	3	5	4
4	3	6	2	9	5	8	1	7
8	7	5	3	4	1	6	9	2
1	9	3	7	8	4	2	6	5
5	8	4	6	2	3	1	7	9
6	2	7	1	5	9	4	8	3

```
T O S I R █ █ H A B
I R E N E S █ S A U L
B A D F I T █ I S N O
I C A L █ E R E S T U
A L T A █ O R L E S █
S E E M █ D A R E M E
█ █ M T I D A █ █ █ █
C A N A R D █ N A G S
A N O T E █ E R A T █
V I S I T S █ V I L A
I M T O █ R E A S O N
E A R N █ S I D E O N
S L A █ S A N T O █
```

AIRLINER

SOLUTIONS

Page 79

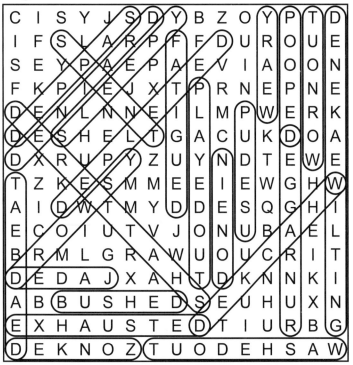

Page 80

8	4	3	6	7	1	9	5	2
7	5	9	3	2	8	1	4	6
2	1	6	4	9	5	7	8	3
1	8	2	5	6	7	4	3	9
3	6	4	2	8	9	5	1	7
9	7	5	1	4	3	2	6	8
4	3	8	7	1	2	6	9	5
6	9	7	8	5	4	3	2	1
5	2	1	9	3	6	8	7	4

7	1	4	8	5	6	9	2	3
3	2	5	1	9	4	8	6	7
6	8	9	7	2	3	1	5	4
4	9	6	3	8	5	2	7	1
8	7	1	9	4	2	5	3	6
5	3	2	6	7	1	4	9	8
1	4	7	5	6	9	3	8	2
2	5	8	4	3	7	6	1	9
9	6	3	2	1	8	7	4	5

Page 81

I	S	H	O	T		F	L	U	K	E
M	E	A	R	A		B	A	R	O	N
P	A	W	A	T		I	G	L	O	O
A	S	T	R	A	L		A	S	K	S
I	N	H	E	R	I	T	S			
R	A	O		S	A	S	E	S		
	K	R	A	F	T	W	E	R	K	
	E	N	T	R	E		E	E	R	
		P	I	N	N	A	C	L	E	
T	H	E	E		S	E	X	T	E	T
H	A	M	A	S		A	M	I	T	E
U	R	I	C	H		T	A	L	O	S
S	P	R	E	E		S	N	E	R	T

Page 82

SWALLOWTAIL
BUTTERFLY

Page 83

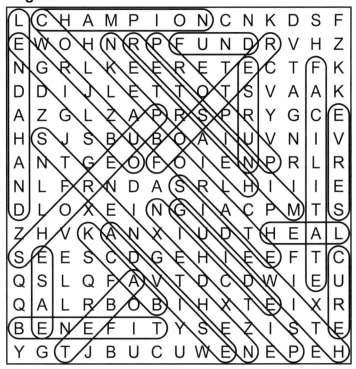

Page 84

4	5	7	2	3	6	1	9	8
1	2	3	4	8	9	5	7	6
9	6	8	5	7	1	4	2	3
5	7	2	9	4	3	8	6	1
8	1	4	7	6	2	3	5	9
6	3	9	1	5	8	7	4	2
2	4	1	3	9	5	6	8	7
7	9	6	8	1	4	2	3	5
3	8	5	6	2	7	9	1	4

3	7	5	4	1	6	9	2	8
8	6	2	9	5	7	1	4	3
4	9	1	2	8	3	6	5	7
6	5	7	3	9	8	4	1	2
2	8	3	1	6	4	7	9	5
9	1	4	7	2	5	8	3	6
5	2	9	6	7	1	3	8	4
1	3	6	8	4	2	5	7	9
7	4	8	5	3	9	2	6	1

Page 85

L	I	F	T	S		L	L	A	M	A
E	N	L	A	I		A	A	R	O	N
S	N	O	R	T		C	Y	C	A	D
H	O	U	S	E	G	U	E	S	T	
	T	R	I	D	E	N	T			
L	I	I		T	A	T	T	O	O	
I	M	S	E	T		R	E	O	R	G
D	E	H	O	R	N		N	A	S	
		L	E	A	F	L	E	T		
	C	H	I	M	N	E	Y	P	O	T
L	I	E	T	O		A	D	O	R	E
S	T	A	H	L		T	I	E	I	N
D	I	D	S	O		S	A	M	O	S

Page 86

DOVE

SOLUTIONS

Page 87

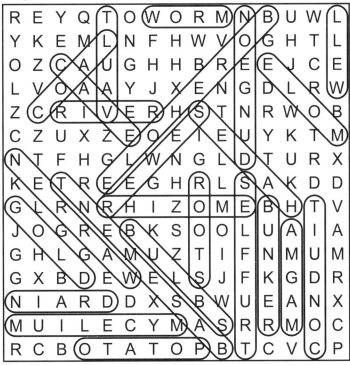

Page 88

9	7	5	6	1	8	2	3	4
4	1	6	3	5	2	7	8	9
3	2	8	7	4	9	1	6	5
2	4	3	1	8	5	6	9	7
7	8	9	2	6	4	5	1	3
6	5	1	9	3	7	8	4	2
1	3	7	5	9	6	4	2	8
8	9	2	4	7	1	3	5	6
5	6	4	8	2	3	9	7	1

4	1	3	7	2	8	5	6	9
6	2	8	9	3	5	1	4	7
7	9	5	6	4	1	8	2	3
8	5	9	4	1	2	3	7	6
1	3	4	5	7	6	9	8	2
2	7	6	3	8	9	4	5	1
5	6	2	8	9	3	7	1	4
9	8	7	1	6	4	2	3	5
3	4	1	2	5	7	6	9	8

Page 89

A	L	B	A	S		C	A	S	E	D
M	A	T	S	U		R	I	C	K	I
S	T	E	P	B	R	O	T	H	E	R
O	E	N		D	O	U	S	E		
			H	U	A	C		D	M	Z
	A	F	T	E	R	H	O	U	R	S
C	L	A	M				E	L	E	A
E	V	I	L	M	I	N	D	E	D	
E	A	L		O	S	I	S			
	S	E	L	I	G		B	A	G	
P	L	A	Y	I	N	G	C	A	R	D
A	D	F	E	E		L	E	E	L	A
R	L	E	S	S		E	L	R	O	Y

Page 90

HORSE

Page 91

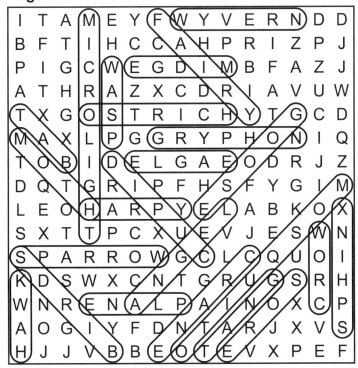

Page 92

6	3	2	5	7	8	9	4	1
1	5	9	2	3	4	7	8	6
8	4	7	9	1	6	3	5	2
9	1	5	3	8	7	2	6	4
7	6	3	4	2	1	5	9	8
2	8	4	6	9	5	1	3	7
3	2	1	8	4	9	6	7	5
4	9	6	7	5	2	8	1	3
5	7	8	1	6	3	4	2	9

8	5	2	1	4	7	6	9	3
6	4	7	3	8	9	2	5	1
1	9	3	5	2	6	4	8	7
5	2	6	4	3	8	1	7	9
9	7	4	6	5	1	8	3	2
3	1	8	9	7	2	5	4	6
4	6	5	2	9	3	7	1	8
2	8	9	7	1	5	3	6	4
7	3	1	8	6	4	9	2	5

Page 93

P	A	L	L		I	N	A	B	I	T
A	V	I	A		M	O	N	R	O	E
R	E	M	O		A	S	T	A	N	A
C	O	N	T	A	G	I	O	U	S	
			S	T	E	R	N			
O	N	E	E	A	R		Y	E	S	T
S	E	M					S	W	E	
U	Z	I	S		T	O	U	C	A	N
		H	A	U	L	S				
	G	R	E	A	T	D	A	N	E	S
B	A	U	B	L	E		U	G	L	Y
O	R	N	A	T	E		S	O	L	S
L	O	T	T	O	S		A	S	E	T

Page 94

PINEAPPLE

243

SOLUTIONS

Page 95

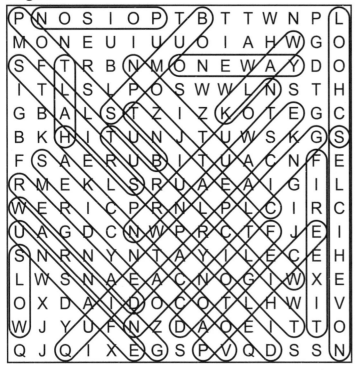

Page 96

7	3	5	1	6	8	9	4	2
4	1	2	5	9	3	8	7	6
9	8	6	2	7	4	3	1	5
5	2	1	8	3	7	6	9	4
6	7	8	4	2	9	1	5	3
3	9	4	6	1	5	7	2	8
8	4	3	9	5	1	2	6	7
2	5	9	7	8	6	4	3	1
1	6	7	3	4	2	5	8	9

6	4	3	5	2	1	8	9	7
9	5	7	3	8	4	2	1	6
8	1	2	7	6	9	4	5	3
7	3	5	6	9	2	1	4	8
2	8	1	4	5	7	6	3	9
3	2	8	9	1	5	7	6	4
1	6	4	2	7	3	9	8	5
5	7	9	8	4	6	3	2	1

Page 97

			T	M	I				
M	A	N		H	E	B		P	T	L
E	C	O	T	A	G	E		L	E	E
O	T	T	O		O	X	C	A	R	T
W	A	H	W	A	H		L	I	R	A
S	S	I		I	M	E	A	N	I	T
		N	O	R		T	Y	S		
A	U	G	M	E	N	T		P	A	L
D	A	N	O		E	U	D	O	R	A
O	N	E	O	N	E		I	K	E	S
S	D	S		E	D	G	I	E	S	T
E	I	S		R	T	E		N	O	S
			F	O	R					

Page 98

SPRINTER

Page 99

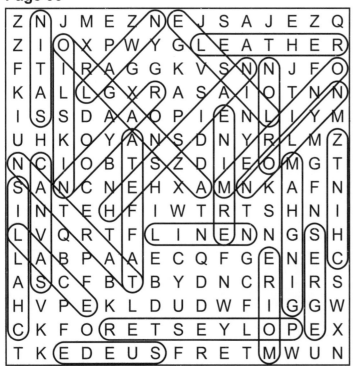

Page 100

6	1	3	4	9	2	8	5	7
7	4	2	8	3	5	6	9	1
9	5	8	6	1	7	4	3	2
8	3	4	2	6	9	1	7	5
1	6	7	3	5	8	9	2	4
2	9	5	7	4	1	3	8	6
3	2	1	9	7	6	5	4	8
4	8	6	5	2	3	7	1	9
5	7	9	1	8	4	2	6	3

1	4	5	8	7	3	2	6	9
2	9	3	4	1	6	5	7	8
6	7	8	9	5	2	1	4	3
8	3	1	7	6	4	9	5	2
7	2	9	5	3	8	4	1	6
5	6	4	1	2	9	8	3	7
3	1	6	2	9	5	7	8	4
9	8	7	6	4	1	3	2	5
4	5	2	3	8	7	6	9	1

Page 101

R	U	R	A	L		C	L	I	M	E
I	N	A	G	E		A	L	S	O	P
E	D	D	I	E	A	L	B	E	R	T
L	O	O	T		C	V	S			
		A	N	C	E		A	C	U	
I	D	O	T	O	O		E	N	O	S
D	E	T	E	R	M	I	N	I	S	M
L	A	R	D		P	I	C	N	I	C
E	R	A		M	A	S	I			
		R	A	N		P	D	A	S	
R	O	T	A	R	Y	P	H	O	N	E
T	I	B	I	A		C	E	S	A	R
S	L	A	N	T		P	R	O	S	E

Page 102

QUEEN ELIZABETH I

SOLUTIONS

Page 103

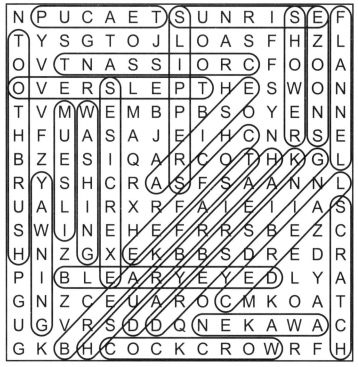

Page 104

8	6	9	1	2	3	4	5	7
2	7	1	5	9	4	6	3	8
5	4	3	8	6	7	9	1	2
3	1	6	2	7	8	5	4	9
4	2	5	9	3	1	8	7	6
7	9	8	6	4	5	1	2	3
1	5	2	7	8	6	3	9	4
6	3	7	4	5	9	2	8	1
9	8	4	3	1	2	7	6	5

7	8	4	5	3	6	1	9	2
9	3	2	1	8	4	7	5	6
6	1	5	7	9	2	3	8	4
2	9	8	3	5	7	6	4	1
3	4	1	2	6	8	5	7	9
5	7	6	4	1	9	2	3	8
8	5	3	6	4	1	9	2	7
4	6	7	9	2	3	8	1	5
1	2	9	8	7	5	4	6	3

Page 105

S	I	B	Y	L			S	M	E	E
M	O	O	M	O	O		M	O	S	S
U	N	S	H	O	D		A	L	T	A
			T	A	N	I	A		L	S	U
S	L	O		Y	U	M	M	Y		
S	E	N	D		M	I	C	R	O	N
G	A	L	O	P		N	A	I	R	A
T	H	E	R	E	S		T	N	T	S
	T	Y	P	E	O		G	S	T	
O	A	T		E	L	B	O	W		
N	E	U	E		M	A	L	A	D	Y
A	R	C	H		A	M	E	L	I	E
N	O	E	S			A	N	D	Y	S

Page 106

ROSE

Page 107

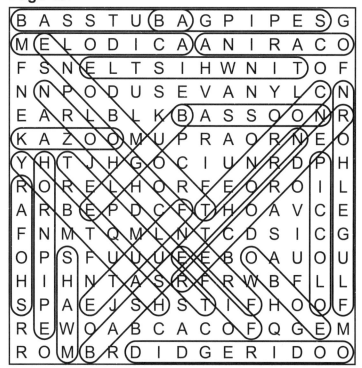

Page 108

3	1	2	9	4	6	5	8	7
9	4	8	5	7	1	3	6	2
5	7	6	2	8	3	9	1	4
7	3	4	1	2	8	6	9	5
2	8	5	4	6	9	1	7	3
1	6	9	7	3	5	2	4	8
4	9	7	6	5	2	8	3	1
8	5	1	3	9	7	4	2	6
6	2	3	8	1	4	7	5	9

5	4	1	9	3	6	7	8	2
9	8	7	5	1	2	6	3	4
6	2	3	7	8	4	5	9	1
8	5	2	1	6	9	4	7	3
1	6	4	3	2	7	9	5	8
3	7	9	8	4	5	2	1	6
7	3	6	2	9	1	8	4	5
2	1	5	4	7	8	3	6	9
4	9	8	6	5	3	1	2	7

Page 109

U	P	A	T			H	A	U	T	E
R	A	D	I	I		A	N	N	E	X
S	I	D	E	S	T	R	O	K	E	S
U	N	E		L	E	D		E	N	T
L	T	R		A	L	P		P	I	A
A	S	S	N		L	U	S	T	E	R
			O	V	A	T	E			
G	O	S	S	I	P		C	A	R	B
A	G	E		S	A	R		C	E	O
R	R	R		C	R	U		C	D	R
L	I	E	D	E	T	E	C	T	O	R
I	S	N	E	R		D	U	N	N	O
C	H	A	K	A			L	O	E	W

Page 110

ANGEL'S TRUMPET

245

SOLUTIONS

Page 111

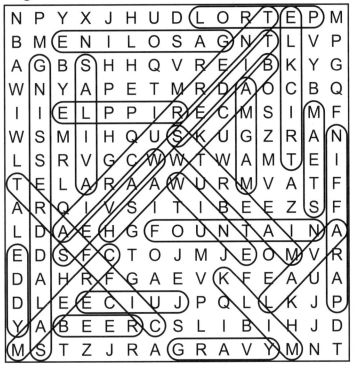

Page 112

5	2	7	3	1	4	8	9	6
8	1	4	9	7	6	3	2	5
9	3	6	5	8	2	1	4	7
7	6	3	8	4	9	5	1	2
2	5	1	7	6	3	4	8	9
4	8	9	1	2	5	6	7	3
3	9	8	4	5	7	2	6	1
1	7	2	6	3	8	9	5	4
6	4	5	2	9	1	7	3	8

6	9	8	7	5	3	4	2	1
3	4	2	8	9	1	6	7	5
5	1	7	4	6	2	3	9	8
1	6	3	9	2	5	7	8	4
7	2	9	6	4	8	1	5	3
8	5	4	3	1	7	2	6	9
2	8	6	5	3	4	9	1	7
9	3	5	1	7	6	8	4	2
4	7	1	2	8	9	5	3	6

Page 113

A	L	S	O	P	■	L	E	C	I	D
B	A	S	S	O	■	I	L	O	N	A
B	I	T	E	T	H	E	D	U	S	T
R	N	S	■	S	E	A	■	G	O	S
■	■	■	T	H	A	T	C	H	■	■
T	Y	D	B	O	L	■	A	I	R	E
P	E	R	O	T	■	O	R	N	A	N
S	T	E	N	■	S	U	N	G	O	D
■	■	A	E	R	A	T	E	■	■	■
A	D	D	■	O	I	L	■	M	A	I
B	U	F	F	A	L	O	B	I	L	L
C	R	U	E	L	■	U	S	E	M	E
D	O	L	E	D	■	D	A	N	A	S

Page 114

GERMAN
SHEPHERD

Page 115

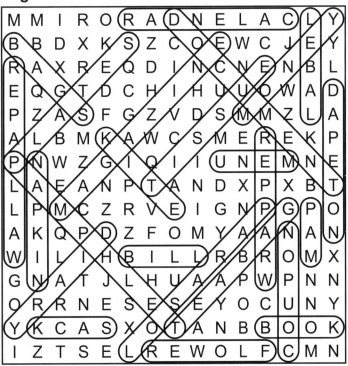

Page 116

8	6	7	4	2	5	3	9	1
5	1	9	8	7	3	6	4	2
3	4	2	6	9	1	7	5	8
1	7	4	3	5	2	8	6	9
6	3	5	9	8	7	2	1	4
9	2	8	1	4	6	5	3	7
4	5	6	2	1	8	9	7	3
7	8	1	5	3	9	4	2	6
2	9	3	7	6	4	1	8	5

6	1	4	8	2	7	5	9	3
8	9	3	5	1	4	7	2	6
7	2	5	3	6	9	8	1	4
1	4	7	9	5	2	6	3	8
9	3	6	1	7	8	4	5	2
5	8	2	6	4	3	9	7	1
4	7	8	2	3	5	1	6	9
2	5	1	4	9	6	3	8	7
3	6	9	7	8	1	2	4	5

Page 117

C	A	G	E	D	■	■	S	A	T	E
I	C	E	B	A	G	■	P	R	E	X
R	E	N	O	I	R	■	I	F	A	T
■	■	E	N	L	I	S	T	■	■	■
S	K	A	■	Y	M	A	■	H	O	T
C	E	L	E	B	■	L	E	E	R	Y
A	M	O	R	E	■	L	E	N	I	N
M	A	G	N	A	■	Y	O	R	B	A
P	L	Y	■	S	W	F	■	I	I	N
■	■	■	O	T	I	O	S	E	■	■
G	A	R	B	■	G	R	O	T	T	O
D	A	D	O	■	S	T	I	T	C	H
S	E	S	E	■	H	E	A	P	S	■

Page 118

ELEPHANT

246

SOLUTIONS

Page 119

Page 120

8	7	5	1	2	4	3	6	9
6	9	3	5	8	7	2	1	4
2	1	4	9	6	3	7	5	8
3	5	2	4	7	6	9	8	1
7	6	1	8	3	9	4	2	5
9	4	8	2	5	1	6	7	3
1	8	6	3	9	2	5	4	7
5	2	9	7	4	8	1	3	6
4	3	7	6	1	5	8	9	2

2	4	7	5	6	8	9	3	1
1	5	3	7	9	4	8	2	6
6	8	9	2	3	1	5	7	4
5	6	8	4	7	3	1	9	2
3	2	1	8	5	9	4	6	7
9	7	4	1	2	6	3	8	5
7	9	5	3	1	2	6	4	8
8	1	6	9	4	7	2	5	3
4	3	2	6	8	5	7	1	9

Page 121

O	C	H	S		A	F	L	A	M	E
L	I	E	U		G	R	I	P	E	R
A	R	A	M		A	E	R	I	A	L
F	O	R	M		S	E	R	E	N	E
		H	O	L	S	T				
O	P	E	N	A	I	R		G	I	S
Y	E	A	S	T		A	F	O	O	T
E	U	R		E	N	D	E	D	U	P
			C	I	E	R	A			
G	O	T	H	O	T		T	W	A	S
E	X	H	U	M	E		I	F	H	E
R	E	A	L	E	R		L	U	S	T
M	S	T	A	R	S		E	L	O	I

Page 122

ALBERT EINSTEIN

Page 123

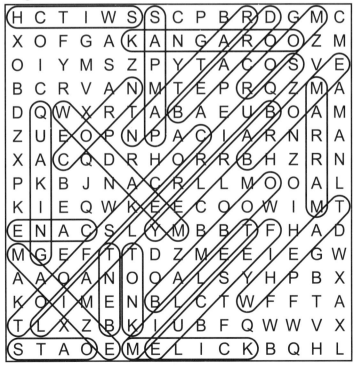

Page 124

5	3	2	1	8	6	4	7	9
4	9	1	3	7	2	5	6	8
6	7	8	5	9	4	3	1	2
9	1	7	4	2	5	6	8	3
8	6	4	7	3	1	9	2	5
2	5	3	9	6	8	7	4	1
1	4	6	8	5	9	2	3	7
7	2	5	6	1	3	8	9	4
3	8	9	2	4	7	1	5	6

7	5	9	2	8	3	1	6	4
1	8	3	4	6	7	9	2	5
2	6	4	5	9	1	3	7	8
4	9	6	7	1	5	8	3	2
8	3	2	9	4	6	7	5	1
5	7	1	8	3	2	4	9	6
3	2	7	1	5	8	6	4	9
9	1	5	6	7	4	2	8	3
6	4	8	3	2	9	5	1	7

Page 125

O	T	E	R	I		U	N	S	E	T
M	A	X	I	M		N	O	E	L	S
E	L	C	A	R		A	K	E	L	A
		O	N	E	C		I	Y	A	R
S	T	M	T		O	R	D	O		
O	H	M		I	N	A	S	U	I	T
I	O	U		L	S	T		I	N	E
R	U	N	R	I	O	T		N	L	E
		I	C	E	R		S	C	A	N
S	N	C	C		T	Y	P	O		
S	E	A	O	F		M	E	U	S	E
T	I	T	L	E		H	A	R	E	D
S	N	E	A	D		A	R	T	S	Y

Page 126

TUTANKHAMUN

SOLUTIONS

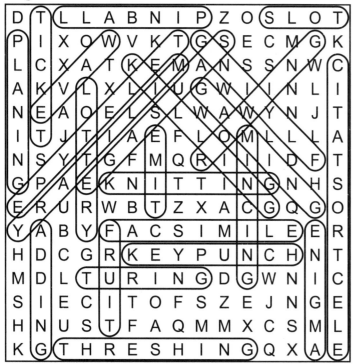

4	2	9	1	5	6	8	7	3
6	8	1	3	7	4	9	5	2
3	5	7	8	9	2	1	6	4
2	1	4	5	8	9	7	3	6
8	9	3	4	6	7	5	2	1
7	6	5	2	3	1	4	8	9
1	4	8	7	2	3	6	9	5
9	7	2	6	1	5	3	4	8
5	3	6	9	4	8	2	1	7

9	6	3	5	7	8	4	2	1
2	5	1	4	3	9	8	7	6
4	7	8	1	2	6	5	3	9
6	8	2	3	4	5	1	9	7
1	3	9	7	8	2	6	4	5
5	4	7	6	9	1	2	8	3
7	2	5	8	1	3	9	6	4
8	1	4	9	6	7	3	5	2
3	9	6	2	5	4	7	1	8

B	E	A	R	D	■	A	M	A	T
A	N	T	R	E	■	A	T	A	R	I
A	F	T	R	A	■	M	C	J	O	B
B	O	A	■	T	H	E	■	O	U	I
A	L	C	O	H	O	L	■	R	S	A
A	D	H	D	■	B	I	N	G	E	S
■	■	■	T	O	N	N	A	G	E	■
A	S	O	N	I	A	■	O	N	C	E
T	I	A	■	H	I	M	S	E	L	F
E	D	W	■	I	L	E	■	R	E	F
S	N	A	R	L	■	R	E	A	V	E
T	E	L	E	O	■	I	N	L	E	T
S	Y	L	L	■	■	T	A	S	S	E

SUNFLOWER

2	4	1	9	6	8	3	7	5
3	9	7	4	5	1	8	6	2
6	5	8	7	3	2	9	1	4
7	2	9	6	1	4	5	3	8
8	6	5	2	7	3	1	4	9
4	1	3	8	9	5	7	2	6
9	8	2	3	4	7	6	5	1
1	7	4	5	8	6	2	9	3
5	3	6	1	2	9	4	8	7

5	7	3	1	4	6	2	9	8
8	4	1	3	2	9	6	7	5
6	2	9	5	8	7	1	3	4
4	8	7	9	5	2	3	1	6
1	6	2	4	7	3	8	5	9
3	9	5	8	6	1	4	2	7
2	3	4	6	9	5	7	8	1
9	1	8	7	3	4	5	6	2
7	5	6	2	1	8	9	4	3

S	H	A	R	P	■	O	F	O	N	E
R	E	N	E	E	■	R	E	B	E	L
T	R	A	C	E	■	I	N	L	A	Y
A	D	D	I	T	I	O	N	A	L	■
■	■	P	E	R	L	E	■	■	■	■
B	O	W	E	■	S	E	L	E	N	A
O	S	S	■	■	■	■	P	A	D	■
S	T	J	O	H	N	■	K	A	N	E
■	■	C	O	A	T	I	■	■	■	■
■	A	N	T	A	G	O	N	I	S	T
O	S	C	A	R	■	E	S	T	E	E
U	N	I	V	S	■	I	K	O	N	S
T	O	S	E	E	■	N	I	N	T	H

CHARLIE CHAPLIN

SOLUTIONS

Page 135

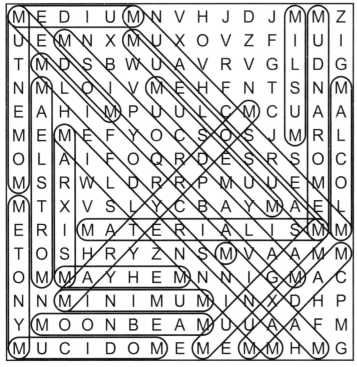

Page 136

8	9	5	2	1	7	3	6	4
7	2	3	4	9	6	1	5	8
1	4	6	8	3	5	9	7	2
6	1	8	9	7	4	2	3	5
5	7	4	3	6	2	8	1	9
9	3	2	1	5	8	7	4	6
3	8	9	6	4	1	5	2	7
2	6	7	5	8	3	4	9	1
4	5	1	7	2	9	6	8	3

6	4	8	2	5	7	3	1	9
3	5	2	1	8	9	6	7	4
9	1	7	3	6	4	5	8	2
7	6	3	4	2	8	9	5	1
1	9	5	7	3	6	4	2	8
2	8	4	9	1	5	7	3	6
4	2	9	8	7	3	1	6	5
5	7	1	6	9	2	8	4	3
8	3	6	5	4	1	2	9	7

Page 137

S	P	O	T	■	I	M	B	E	A	T
T	U	N	A	■	M	A	L	A	G	A
O	P	E	N	■	P	O	I	S	E	S
A	U	L	D	■	A	R	N	E	S	S
■	■	■	E	L	C	I	D	■	■	■
S	U	M	M	I	T	■	M	E	A	L
B	R	I	B	E	■	C	A	C	H	E
A	L	I	I	■	J	I	N	G	L	E
■	■	■	C	B	E	R	S	■	■	■
P	R	E	Y	O	N	■	B	I	D	E
O	I	L	C	A	N	■	U	S	E	E
S	V	E	L	T	E	■	F	A	Y	E
T	A	M	E	S	T	■	F	O	S	S

Page 138

FORD MUSTANG

Page 139

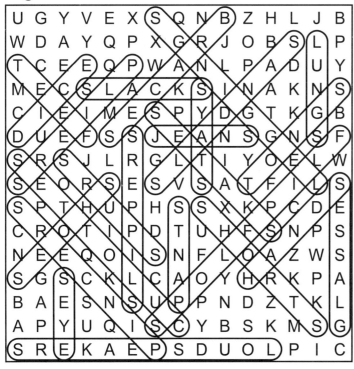

Page 140

4	8	1	9	3	2	7	5	6
6	3	5	7	8	1	9	4	2
7	2	9	6	5	4	8	1	3
1	7	6	2	4	9	5	3	8
3	5	4	8	7	6	1	2	9
2	9	8	3	1	5	4	6	7
9	4	7	5	2	3	6	8	1
8	1	3	4	6	7	2	9	5
5	6	2	1	9	8	3	7	4

4	5	8	9	2	6	3	1	7
2	3	6	5	1	7	9	8	4
7	1	9	4	3	8	6	2	5
3	7	1	2	6	5	8	4	9
6	2	5	8	4	9	7	3	1
9	8	4	1	7	3	2	5	6
5	6	7	3	8	4	1	9	2
8	4	2	7	9	1	5	6	3
1	9	3	6	5	2	4	7	8

Page 141

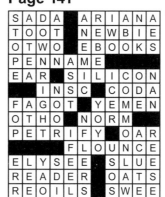

S	A	D	A	■	A	R	I	A	N	A
T	O	O	T	■	N	E	W	B	I	E
O	T	W	O	■	E	B	O	O	K	S
P	E	N	N	A	M	E	■	■	■	■
E	A	R	■	S	I	L	I	C	O	N
■	■	■	I	N	S	C	■	C	O	D	A
F	A	G	O	T	■	Y	E	M	E	N
O	T	H	O	■	N	O	R	M	■	■
P	E	T	R	I	F	Y	■	O	A	R
■	■	■	F	L	O	U	N	C	E	
E	L	Y	S	E	E	■	S	L	U	E
R	E	A	D	E	R	■	O	A	T	S
R	E	O	I	L	S	■	S	W	E	E

Page 142

TORTOISE

249

SOLUTIONS

Page 143

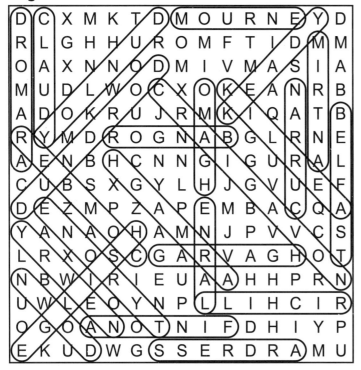

Page 144

6	4	5	7	8	2	9	3	1
8	2	1	4	9	3	6	5	7
9	3	7	6	5	1	2	4	8
4	6	3	2	1	8	7	9	5
1	9	8	5	4	7	3	2	6
7	5	2	3	6	9	1	8	4
3	1	4	9	7	5	8	6	2
5	7	9	8	2	6	4	1	3
2	8	6	1	3	4	5	7	9

9	7	2	4	6	8	5	1	3
6	4	8	5	3	1	7	2	9
3	5	1	7	9	2	4	8	6
8	6	7	3	1	4	9	5	2
2	9	5	6	8	7	3	4	1
1	3	4	9	2	5	6	7	8
7	8	9	1	4	6	2	3	5
4	1	6	2	5	3	8	9	7
5	2	3	8	7	9	1	6	4

Page 145

S	I	N	■	L	I	C	■	H	O	P
A	L	E	■	I	N	A	■	A	T	L
V	I	A	D	U	C	T	■	N	E	U
E	E	R	O	■	I	C	E	D	A	M
■	■	W	A	S	H	U	P	■	■	■
S	I	G	N	E	E	■	R	I	T	T
C	L	E	F	S	■	B	O	C	C	I
I	O	N	A	■	N	A	P	K	I	N
■	■	■	I	L	L	I	N	I	■	■
J	E	T	L	A	G	■	U	L	E	E
U	R	I	■	R	H	O	M	B	U	S
L	I	V	■	G	O	D	■	O	L	E
Y	E	E	■	O	N	E	■	S	A	S

Page 146

IRIS

Page 147

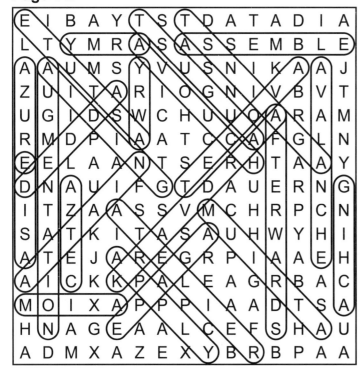

Page 148

1	3	6	8	5	9	4	2	7
5	9	2	7	4	1	6	8	3
7	4	8	3	6	2	9	5	1
4	2	5	6	8	3	1	7	9
3	7	9	2	1	5	8	6	4
6	8	1	4	9	7	2	3	5
2	5	4	1	7	8	3	9	6
8	1	7	9	3	6	5	4	2
9	6	3	5	2	4	7	1	8

5	6	2	9	8	3	7	1	4
7	1	3	4	5	6	8	2	9
9	8	4	2	1	7	6	3	5
1	5	7	6	4	2	3	9	8
3	9	8	1	7	5	4	6	2
4	2	6	3	9	8	1	5	7
6	4	5	7	2	1	9	8	3
2	3	9	8	6	4	5	7	1
8	7	1	5	3	9	2	4	6

Page 149

H	A	C	K	■	A	D	M	I	R	E
A	L	I	A	■	M	E	A	T	A	X
V	E	G	A	■	B	A	T	T	L	E
O	R	A	■	L	I	R	R	■	■	■
C	O	R	E	A	■	L	I	O	N	S
■	■	E	N	C	■	Y	A	X	I	S
N	O	T	E	■	■	■	R	Y	N	E
I	N	T	R	O	■	A	C	C	■	■
L	I	E	G	E	■	G	H	O	U	L
■	■	E	U	L	A	■	N	H	A	■
P	A	R	T	V	I	■	S	T	U	D
T	H	E	I	R	S	■	A	I	R	Y
L	A	N	C	E	T	■	O	N	U	S

Page 150

STAG BEETLE

250

SOLUTIONS

Page 151

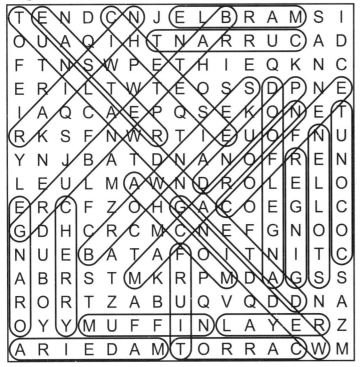

Page 152

5	6	2	1	3	7	8	9	4
1	7	3	9	8	4	2	5	6
9	4	8	5	2	6	3	1	7
3	5	7	8	4	1	6	2	9
8	1	4	2	6	9	7	3	5
2	9	6	3	7	5	4	8	1
4	3	1	6	9	8	5	7	2
6	8	9	7	5	2	1	4	3
7	2	5	4	1	3	9	6	8

2	3	7	6	8	1	9	5	4
8	1	6	5	4	9	3	7	2
4	9	5	7	2	3	1	6	8
3	5	2	8	1	7	6	4	9
1	7	8	4	9	6	5	2	3
9	6	4	2	3	5	7	8	1
5	4	3	1	7	2	8	9	6
7	2	1	9	6	8	4	3	5
6	8	9	3	5	4	2	1	7

Page 153

T	E	L	A	V	I	V	■	S	E	L
A	M	E	R	I	C	A	■	A	S	I
J	O	K	E	S	O	N	■	I	S	L
■	■	■	T	O	N	I	■	L	I	A
A	B	H	O	R	■	L	E	B	E	C
E	C	O	■	■	C	L	E	O	■	■
R	E	P	E	A	T	A	G	A	I	N
■	■	E	T	C	S	■	■	R	S	A
U	L	C	E	R	■	S	A	D	H	E
D	U	H	■	E	D	H	S	■	■	■
A	C	E	■	A	R	A	P	A	H	O
L	I	S	■	G	E	M	I	N	I	S
L	E	T	■	E	D	U	C	A	T	E

Page 154

EAGLE HEAD

Page 155

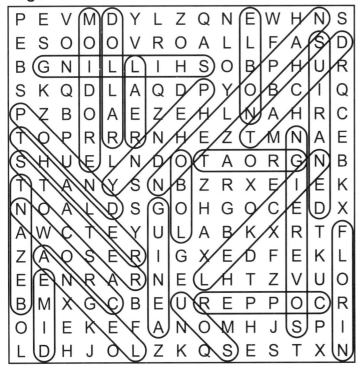

Page 156

9	2	4	3	7	8	1	6	5
8	6	3	5	9	1	2	7	4
1	5	7	6	4	2	3	9	8
7	4	9	2	8	6	5	3	1
3	1	2	4	5	7	9	8	6
6	8	5	1	3	9	4	2	7
2	9	6	8	1	5	7	4	3
5	3	8	7	2	4	6	1	9
4	7	1	9	6	3	8	5	2

6	9	4	7	5	3	2	8	1
1	3	8	2	4	6	5	7	9
7	2	5	8	1	9	3	4	6
5	7	1	3	9	8	6	2	4
2	4	6	1	7	5	8	9	3
9	8	3	4	6	2	1	5	7
3	6	2	9	8	4	7	1	5
4	5	7	6	2	1	9	3	8
8	1	9	5	3	7	4	6	2

Page 157

A	Q	U	A	S	■	I	N	F	O	■
P	I	P	P	A	■	M	E	A	N	A
A	N	T	I	C	I	P	A	T	E	D
C	T	U	■	R	N	A	■	I	C	E
H	A	R	N	E	S	S	■	M	A	E
E	R	N	O	■	T	S	G	A	R	P
■	■	A	D	I	E	U	■	■	■	■
O	R	C	H	I	L	■	L	S	A	T
L	E	A	■	O	L	D	L	I	N	E
E	D	M	■	C	E	E	■	E	D	A
G	R	A	V	E	D	I	G	G	E	R
S	E	R	E	S	■	S	H	E	R	A
■	W	O	R	E	■	M	I	D	S	T

Page 158

PANDA

251

SOLUTIONS

Page 159

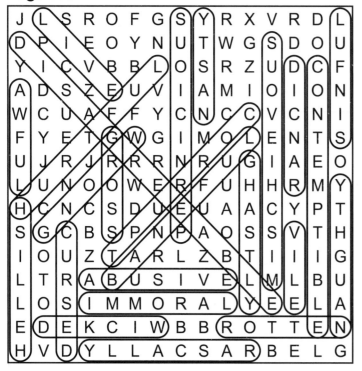

Page 160

2	4	9	8	3	1	6	7	5
7	5	6	4	2	9	8	1	3
1	3	8	5	7	6	4	9	2
8	1	3	7	6	5	2	4	9
6	7	5	2	9	4	3	8	1
9	2	4	3	1	8	5	6	7
4	9	2	1	8	3	7	5	6
5	6	7	9	4	2	1	3	8
3	8	1	6	5	7	9	2	4

2	3	9	6	4	7	1	5	8
8	7	5	1	2	9	4	6	3
1	6	4	8	5	3	9	2	7
3	9	7	5	1	2	8	4	6
6	5	8	9	7	4	3	1	2
4	1	2	3	8	6	7	9	5
9	8	3	2	6	1	5	7	4
7	2	1	4	3	5	6	8	9
5	4	6	7	9	8	2	3	1

Page 161

M	A	C	A	W	■	S	A	J	A	K
I	S	I	A	H	■	L	L	A	M	A
A	P	P	R	O	B	A	T	I	O	N
M	E	H	■	P	U	P	■	L	U	S
I	C	E	■	P	T	S	■	E	N	A
S	T	R	E	E	T	■	O	R	T	S
■	■	■	C	R	E	D	O	■	■	■
P	E	N	H	■	R	E	F	F	E	D
I	N	O	■	P	F	C	■	I	N	U
F	U	N	■	E	L	I	■	N	O	R
F	R	E	A	K	Y	D	E	A	K	Y
L	E	T	M	E	■	E	L	L	I	E
E	S	S	E	S	■	D	O	E	S	A

Page 162

FRENCH HORN

Page 163

Page 164

3	7	1	2	5	8	4	9	6
9	2	6	3	4	7	1	8	5
4	5	8	1	6	9	7	3	2
6	4	3	7	8	5	9	2	1
5	1	2	4	9	3	6	7	8
7	8	9	6	2	1	5	4	3
2	6	5	8	7	4	3	1	9
8	3	7	9	1	6	2	5	4
1	9	4	5	3	2	8	6	7

4	2	7	3	1	6	5	9	8
5	9	3	7	2	8	4	1	6
1	6	8	9	4	5	7	3	2
9	1	5	4	6	2	3	8	7
2	8	4	1	3	7	9	6	5
3	7	6	5	8	9	1	2	4
7	5	2	6	9	1	8	4	3
8	3	9	2	5	4	6	7	1
6	4	1	8	7	3	2	5	9

Page 165

M	I	D	S	T	■	B	Y	R	O	N
O	N	E	T	O	■	U	A	N	D	I
A	T	S	E	A	■	F	L	A	I	L
B	L	O	W	S	A	F	U	S	E	■
■	■	■	L	O	T	S	A	■	■	■
S	L	A	V	■	A	L	S	A	C	E
A	O	T	E	A	■	O	U	T	G	O
O	P	E	R	A	S	■	R	H	I	N
■	■	■	M	O	D	E	L	■	■	■
■	D	E	F	I	N	I	T	E	L	Y
T	R	I	A	L	■	T	I	T	A	N
M	A	R	I	N	■	K	E	E	N	E
I	W	E	R	E	■	A	S	S	E	Z

Page 166

DRUM HORSE

SOLUTIONS

Page 167

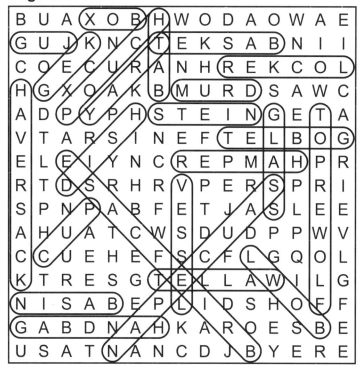

Page 168

9	4	3	5	8	1	6	7	2
2	6	8	4	3	7	9	5	1
5	1	7	6	2	9	3	8	4
3	5	6	7	9	4	2	1	8
1	2	4	8	5	6	7	9	3
8	7	9	2	1	3	5	4	6
7	3	2	9	4	8	1	6	5
4	9	5	1	6	2	8	3	7
6	8	1	3	7	5	4	2	9

6	9	8	3	7	2	1	5	4
4	3	5	9	1	8	7	6	2
1	7	2	4	6	5	3	9	8
7	4	9	5	8	3	2	1	6
8	2	1	6	9	4	5	7	3
5	6	3	7	2	1	8	4	9
9	5	7	8	3	6	4	2	1
2	8	4	1	5	9	6	3	7
3	1	6	2	4	7	9	8	5

Page 169

M	O	U	S	Y	█	C	O	Z	E	N
M	I	N	E	O	█	I	V	A	N	A
E	L	F	I	N	█	R	O	C	C	O
█	█	O	S	K	A	R	█	H	E	S
A	I	R	█	E	L	I	Z	A	█	█
C	S	T	O	R	E	█	O	R	A	N
D	A	U	B	S	█	R	O	Y	K	O
C	O	N	E	█	W	E	S	T	I	E
█	█	A	Y	E	A	R	█	A	N	S
D	E	T	█	P	R	O	S	Y	█	█
A	C	E	T	O	█	U	H	L	A	N
R	U	L	E	D	█	T	O	O	L	E
C	A	Y	C	E	█	E	E	R	I	E

Page 170

GIRL WITH A PEARL EARRING

Page 171

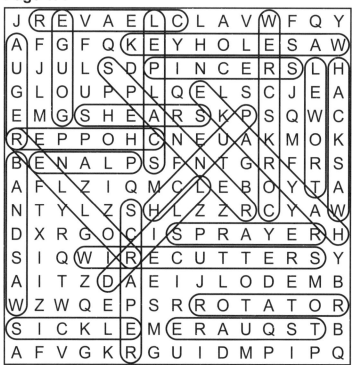

Page 172

3	4	5	7	1	2	8	6	9
9	1	7	6	8	5	4	3	2
8	2	6	4	9	3	1	5	7
2	9	8	5	4	6	3	7	1
7	6	1	2	3	9	5	8	4
5	3	4	1	7	8	2	9	6
4	5	9	3	2	7	6	1	8
6	7	2	8	5	1	9	4	3
1	8	3	9	6	4	7	2	5

3	7	9	1	5	4	6	8	2
1	4	6	8	9	2	7	3	5
2	8	5	6	3	7	1	9	4
9	3	7	4	8	5	2	1	6
6	5	2	3	1	9	4	7	8
4	1	8	7	2	6	3	5	9
8	9	3	2	4	1	5	6	7
7	2	1	5	6	8	9	4	3
5	6	4	9	7	3	8	2	1

Page 173

R	A	S	█	A	A	M	█	F	A	S
A	Z	T	█	L	B	O	█	A	R	P
T	A	R	█	G	E	L	█	T	R	A
E	L	I	█	A	D	O	P	T	E	R
D	E	N	S	E	█	█	K	A	Y	A	K
R	A	G	U	█	C	A	N	A	R	Y
█	█	B	A	W	D	I	E	R	█	█
O	S	I	R	I	S	█	█	R	B	I	S
B	A	K	E	D	█	S	A	U	C	E
R	H	I	Z	O	M	E	█	C	O	X
I	A	N	█	W	I	I	█	K	N	T
E	R	I	█	E	L	K	█	L	I	E
N	A	S	█	R	A	O	█	E	C	T

Page 174

GOLDEN HIND

253

SOLUTIONS

Page 175

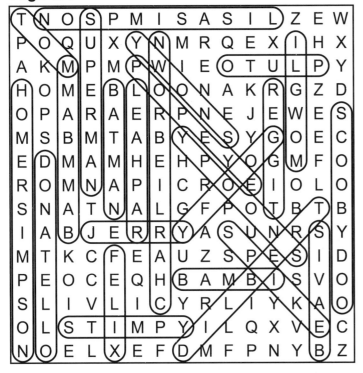

Page 176

9	4	3	6	7	5	8	2	1
5	1	7	3	8	2	9	4	6
2	8	6	9	1	4	7	3	5
1	9	2	5	6	7	3	8	4
4	3	8	2	9	1	5	6	7
6	7	5	4	3	8	1	9	2
7	2	4	8	5	3	6	1	9
3	5	9	1	2	6	4	7	8
8	6	1	7	4	9	2	5	3

4	2	1	6	8	7	3	5	9
5	9	8	3	1	2	6	4	7
6	7	3	5	4	9	1	2	8
8	6	7	2	9	3	5	1	4
1	4	9	8	6	5	7	3	2
3	5	2	4	7	1	8	9	6
2	8	6	1	3	4	9	7	5
9	3	5	7	2	8	4	6	1
7	1	4	9	5	6	2	8	3

Page 177

B	E	R	M			D	O	E	S	A
A	S	E	A		D	I	N	G	H	Y
U	S	M	C		O	M	E	G	A	S
M	E	I	R		R	E	A	R	M	
	S	T	A	S	I		D	O	P	E
	M	P	A	A		L	O	A		
O	R	D	E	R		T	A	L	O	N
E	O	E		S	I	T	N			
D	U	M	B		B	U	Y	U	P	
	L	E	I	L	A		B	N	A	I
J	A	R	J	A	R		O	J	O	S
I	D	I	O	T	S		D	A	L	E
F	E	T	U	S			Y	M	I	R

Page 178

"FRIEND" SIGNAGE

Page 179

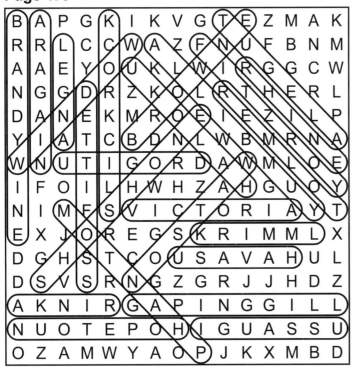

Page 180

8	9	5	6	7	2	4	1	3
4	2	6	3	9	1	5	7	8
7	3	1	4	5	8	2	9	6
5	4	2	7	8	9	6	3	1
1	7	3	5	4	6	9	8	2
6	8	9	2	1	3	7	4	5
2	1	8	9	6	4	3	5	7
3	5	4	8	2	7	1	6	9
9	6	7	1	3	5	8	2	4

6	9	4	1	7	8	3	5	2
3	2	8	6	5	4	7	9	1
1	7	5	9	2	3	6	4	8
8	3	9	4	6	7	2	1	5
5	1	7	2	3	9	4	8	6
2	4	6	5	8	1	9	7	3
9	8	1	3	4	2	5	6	7
4	6	3	7	1	5	8	2	9
7	5	2	8	9	6	1	3	4

Page 181

B	I	T	T	E	R		I	P	O	D
I	T	R	I	E	D		T	A	D	A
P	A	E	L	L	A		S	N	O	T
		E	E	E		M	A	G	M	A
A	L	F		D	D	A	Y			
N	I	E		R	E	S	E	E	K	
A	E	R		B	I	S		S	R	A
S	U	N	K	E	N		P	E	N	
			I	L	K	A		O	B	S
G	A	L	B	A		T	O	S		
O	L	I	O		T	U	N	I	C	S
T	E	N	S		C	R	E	T	I	N
A	R	C	H		U	N	C	O	I	L

Page 182

TELECASTER

SOLUTIONS

Page 183

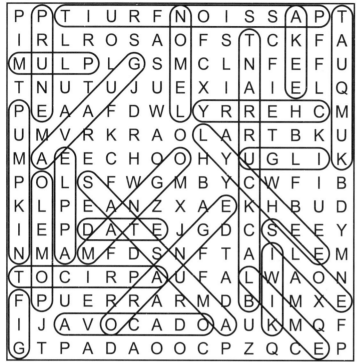

Page 184

6	1	4	3	5	9	7	2	8
8	7	3	2	4	6	1	9	5
2	9	5	7	1	8	4	3	6
3	5	9	6	7	4	2	8	1
1	8	2	9	3	5	6	4	7
7	4	6	1	8	2	9	5	3
4	3	7	5	9	1	8	6	2
5	2	8	4	6	7	3	1	9
9	6	1	8	2	3	5	7	4

9	8	3	2	1	7	4	5	6
5	7	2	6	3	4	8	9	1
6	4	1	5	9	8	2	3	7
1	5	7	9	8	3	6	4	2
8	3	4	1	6	2	5	7	9
2	6	9	7	4	5	1	8	3
3	1	5	8	2	9	7	6	4
4	2	8	3	7	6	9	1	5
7	9	6	4	5	1	3	2	8

Page 185

255